D1001176

B-52 STRATOFORTRESS

U.S. AIR FORCE

B-52 STRATOFORTRESS

Jeff Ethell & Joe Christy

Charles Scribner's Sons
NEW YORK

First U.S. edition published by
Charles Scribner's Sons 1981

1 3 5 7 9 11 13 15 17 19 I/C 20 18 16 14 12 10 8 6 4 2

Printed in Great Britain

Library of Congress Catalog Card Number 81-50153
ISBN: 0-684-16980-0

Contents

Preface

If ever the United States Air Force ordered an aeroplane largely on faith alone, that aeroplane was the B-52 strategic bomber. As things turned out, seldom has such faith been so well placed.

Studying now-declassified secret reports on the B-52 concepts (there were several), and the manner in which those ideas evolved, one must admire the boldness inherent in this highly expensive gamble. True, the design studies appeared sound, and the ultimate 'paper aeroplane' seemed reasonably feasible. Nevertheless, the early documents clearly reveal that the true philosophy behind the project was, simply, 'This is what we must have, therefore it must succeed'.

That, my fellow aeronauts, is faith.

As this is written, the B-52 is in its third decade of operational service with America's Strategic Air Command, and the Air Force says that the 300 remaining in active inventory are expected to be operational for the rest of this century. If this does indeed prove to be the case then, surely, the B-52 will have to be regarded as the most successful military aircraft ever built.

The Air Force predicates the above expectation upon the assumption that the B-52s of the 1980s and 1990s will be fitted with ever more advanced weaponry and electronic countermeasures systems. At this writing, such weaponry is represented by the promise of the Air Launched Cruise Missile (ALCM), which may be released at much greater distances from the target than the Short Range Attack Missile (SRAM) currently carried.

However, there is no guarantee that the cruise missile will be deployed. It appears to be a bargaining chip in the Strategic Arms Limitation Talks with the Soviets and could be traded away. That, in turn, could markedly affect the future effectiveness of the B-52 as Soviet defences steadily improve.

Right: The Boeing YB-52, one of two prototypes of the 742 Stratofortresses to follow. Few people could have forseen that a design concept begun in the 1940s would lead to a bomber destined to form the backbone of US strategic airpower from the late 1950s seemingly into infinity. *Boeing*

9231
UNITED STATES AIR FORCE
BOEING
YB-52
STRATOFORTRESS

The B-52's gestation period was long and painful because its Boeing engineering team had to meet some rather incredible specifications. Boeing was, in effect, expected to design an aeroplane that logically should not have appeared for at least another 10 years. The result was not only a tribute to the bold genius of key Boeing people, but also to the vision and high competence of the USAF officers who patiently nursed and defended the programme through years of frustration. Yea, verily, there were giants in those days.

The B-52 had to come from Boeing. In the mid-1940s, shortly after the end of World War 2, only two other US airframe builders were willing to commit themselves to such a large and uncertain project in the face of massive cuts in military spending. These were Northrop and Convair. However, the Northrop 'Flying Wing' encountered unique problems with no certain solutions; and Convair, preoccupied with its B-36 programme, clung too long to the belief that its version of a B-52 would essentially be a re-engined B-36. At Boeing, the challenge was met with enthusiasm and a clean sheet of paper for an all-new design.

The enthusiasm was sorely tried during the next three years, and a lot of paper went into engineering wastebaskets; but the strange behemoth that slowly evolved from such effort was a totally logical jet-age successor to the B-17 and B-29. It would have been unseemly indeed had it been anything but a Boeing.

Although the company founded in Seattle, Washington by William E. Boeing in 1916 had been building military aircraft from the beginning, its only bomber design prior to the B-17 (except for Navy patrol boats) was the B-9 of 1931, which was as advanced for its time as the B-52 would be 25 years later. The all-metal, twin-engine B-9 was not accepted by the Army Air Corps. It was the first modern US bomber, offered as a replacement for the fabric-covered Keystone biplanes, but a couple of years later, while the Air Corps was still evaluating the B-9, the Martin B-10 appeared with all the same features (cantilever monoplane, retractable landing gear, internal bomb stowage) plus better performance. So, the Air Corps bought the B-10.

The Boeing B-17 prototype, model 299, followed in 1935, and though General H.H. 'Hap' Arnold insisted that it was purely a 'defensive' weapon (surely, with his fingers crossed behind him), the isolationists in the US Congress and the saddle-horse US Army general staff were suspicious, and America's first strategic bomber was not ordered in meaningful numbers until mid-1941, a scant few months before the US was plunged into World War 2.

After the war, opposition to the B-52 – partly within the USAF itself – left its acquisition similarly in doubt, until the Soviets unwisely, though unmistakably, proved the need for it.

Acknowledgements

For the most part the full story of the B-52 has been hidden in the past and without a great deal of help, this book would have had far less scope. The authors have been privileged to uncover most of the BUFF's story in detective story fashion from original development documents to current SAC operations

. . . but through many researchers, pilots and Air Force personnel.

Maj Paul K. Kahl, Sr, USAF, Chief, Magazine & Book Division, Department of the Air Force gave his full support in obtaining photographs and information from in-house sources. Robert J. Smith, Chief, Office of History, HQ Air Force Logistics Command opened the vast documents section that contained the complete development story of the B-52 that had been so elusive. Charles G. Worman and Royal Frey of the Air Force Museum made a point of opening the files in the Museum's excellent research centre.

At HQ Strategic Air Command, Offutt AFB, Nebraska Col David O. Schillerstrom, Director of Information; Maj Allan C. Viguerie, Chief, Audio-Visual Branch and Maj Larry Brown were my hosts for a full series of briefings on and future plans for the B-52, both photographically and in documentary form. James N. Eastman, Jr, Chief, Research Branch, Albert F. Simpson Historical Research Center, USAF, Maxwell AFB, Alabama pointed the authors to several sources of the B-52's combat career.

H. D. Hollinger at Boeing Wichita, where most of the B-52s were built, opened the company's files for data and photos. Peter M. Bowers, long a Boeing employee at Boeing Seattle, came through with a great deal from his extensive personal archives.

The many pilots and crew members who knew the BUFF both in the air and on the ground made the service history of the aircraft come alive. Without their help, the much needed glimpse into what things were like from the participants' side would have been impossible to cover. Our very warmest to Dana Drenkowski, Bob Johnson, Bob Jacober, Tom Dorsey, Vince Osborne, Geoff Engels and Rick Millikin.

And certainly the most intimate glimpse into the aircraft was the opportunity to fly it two times with the 68th Bombardment Wing, 51st Bomb Squadron at Seymour Johnson AFB, North Carolina. The hospitality and the missions were outstanding – all our best to wing commanders Col Caryl Calhoun and Col Henry Conn, 51st Commander Col Francis Hamilton, aircraft commanders Lt-Col Hugh Wellford and Maj Hugh Nixon, Jr and to all of you in the 68th and in SAC who work so hard at making the BUFF an effective weapon system.

To all you BUFF drivers . . . Falcon Code 199!

Left: Boeing have produced a series of strategic bombers for the US air forces. The first combat-ready B-17 was the E model which entered production late in 1941. Pictured are B-17Gs of the 96th Bomb Group, last of the series. A total of 10,731 B-17s were built by Boeing, Douglas (Vega) and Lockheed. *Above:* The Boeing B-29 Superfortress, successor to the B-17, flew for the first time in September 1942. It was the first pressurised bomber. The design was laid down in 1940, and by mid-1944 B-29s were bombing Japan from bases in China. A total of 3,960 were built by Boeing, Bell and Martin. *USAF*

Yet Another Fortress

The B-52 concept evolved on paper over a period of several years. Most USAF leaders knew all along what they wanted, but found themselves funding a series of expensive design studies that fell short of the mark while waiting for engines that would provide the required performance.

This was an old story. Even the Wright brothers were forced to delay demonstration of the world's first successful aeroplane while they designed and built a suitable engine for it. Development of aircraft propulsion systems have set the pace of aeronautical progress ever since.

While the B-52 was still in the idea stage its proponents were faced with another problem. Not everyone believed in the global bomber concept. The B-52 was envisioned as the machine that would replace the B-36 in the late 1950s; but meanwhile the B-36 was having a hard time getting off the ground due to powerful opposition within the Air Force.

The B-36 was actually a World War 2 design, originally contracted in October 1941. This programme, however, simmered on a back burner during the war and was not revived until 1946. Then, it was mid-1948 before the full programme to produce 100 of these giants was at last approved, primarily because of the disagreement between Gen George Kenney, commander of the Strategic Air Command (SAC), who opposed the global bomber concept, and Gen Carl 'Tooey' Spaatz, USAF Chief of Staff, who favoured it. Standing with Kenney in the controversy was Gen Lauris Norstad, USAF Deputy Chief of Staff for Operations.

This squabble spilled over into the B-52 project, and at one point – in January 1948 – the B-52 engineering study was stopped and plans made to build only a few B-36s as aerial tankers for the B-50. Kenney and Norstad had prevailed.

Kenney and Norstad, of course, appeared to have a strong position. America was the sole possessor of the A-bomb which made another major war highly unlikely. In any case, the USAF would have overseas bases for its strategic bombers, and the less costly B-50 (essentially, the B-29 with more powerful engines) could be spread around in greater numbers.

However, 1948 proved to be a year of awakening for any who believed that Russian ambitions had been satisfied with the rape of Eastern Europe and the looting of Russian-occupied Germany. Russia's brazen blockade of West Berlin brought the character of Soviet Communism into sharp focus, and America's intercontinental bomber projects were suddenly viewed in a different light. The blockade of West Berlin began on 24 June 1948, and the next day, USAF brass, headed by Gen Hoyt Vandenberg (appointed Air Force Chief of Staff two months earlier upon Gen Spaatz's retirement), met with Air Force Secretary Stuart Symington and determined that a fleet of B-36 bombers would be built. Generals Kenney and Norstad reversed their previous stand to make the decision unanimous.

The Cold War era ushered in by the Berlin blockade, and Russia's acquisition of nuclear weapons, along with a communist take-over in China, ensured that a force of B-52s would soon follow the B-36s.

During the two and a half years preceding the Berlin blockade, the Boeing Company made several engineering studies of straight-wing prop-jets in response to the B-52 requirement. The first of these, Model 462, offered early in 1946, greatly resembled the B-36 with tractor instead of pusher engines. If built, it would have a wingspan of 221ft, an all-up weight of 360,000lb, an estimated range of 6,200 miles at 410mph, and its engines would be the then-experimental Wright XT-35.

The Air Force was not long in deciding that such a craft would be too slow, too heavy and too late, with little performance advantage over the B-36. Boeing was informed accordingly by General E.E. Partridge, Assistant Chief of Air Staff-3, and Boeing engineers started over with a clean sheet of paper.

The next proposal was for a four-engine craft which would possess certain characteristics recommended by Gen Curtis E. 'Iron Butt' LeMay, then Air Force Deputy Chief of Staff for Research and Development. This proposal was ready in December 1946, and suggested two versions, Models 464-16 and -17. The latter would have a 10,000-mile range with a 10,000lb bomb capacity (a nuclear carrier), and the former would be a 'general purpose' bomber of lesser range but with a bomb capacity of 90,000lb. Gross weight was up to 480,000lb, and cruising speed at 35,000ft was projected at 400mph.

The Air Force again protested that this was much too slow, pointing out that a high-altitude intercontinental bomber should have a speed no less than 25% below that of enemy interceptors. The theory behind this figure was that enemy fighters possessing a speed advantage of no more than 25%

Above: The Boeing B-50 was the inevitable B-29 follow-on pending development of new jet engines. Stronger 75ST skin and more powerful engines resulted in a significantly superior aeroplane to the B-29. This B-50 has just released a Bell X-2 experimental rocket plane over Edwards AFB in July 1956. An early model F-86 serves as chase plane. *USAF*

could not reach such a bomber force in time to prevent it from accomplishing its mission (assuming 30 minutes' advance warning). There would seem to be a couple of important variables in this equation, but it did represent Air Force thinking at the time.

By this time it was clear that the Air Force was going to have to accept a very heavy airplane if it was to have both the range and speed desired. Reluctantly, in February 1947, more money was released to Boeing to continue engineering studies of the Model 464-17 10,000-mile prop-jet. Everyone knew this was not the final answer, but it was the only answer they had at this point. The prop-jet continued to receive serious consideration because there was no pure jet engine of sufficient power on the horizon, and because the prop-jet promised much better fuel economy, which of course translated into greater range. It seems apparent that the problems attendant to propeller design for high-altitude high-speed flight were not fully recognised at that time.

Perhaps one reason the Air Force stuck by Boeing through this series of deficient proposals was the much happier promise offered by the new Boeing B-47 Stratojet, the prototype of which was then under

construction. With a design weight of 125,000lb, and powered with six General Electric J47 turbo-jets of 5,000lb static thrust, the B-47 medium bomber had a projected speed of 600mph and a range of 3,000 miles.

Meanwhile, with so many cooks stirring the B-52 pot there was no dearth of ideas. Many armament and crew configurations were considered, and for a time Boeing recommended an auxiliary landing gear that could be jettisoned after take-off. Dual-rotating propellers were planned for the ultimate prop-jet version, although that, too, required a special development programme. Therefore, the prop-jet B-52 was, for the time being, planned with 23ft four-blade single-rotating propellers.

The new Model 464-25 was offered to the Air Force in March 1947. It had a bicycle type landing gear (similar to that of the B-47) consisting of four dual wheels in tandem with one dual wheel outrigger on each wing. This design also had an extended dorsal fin, and an all-new wing with tapered leading edge. Changes to this design apparently resulted in the Model 464-29, presented in August 1947. Boeing sources briefly mention a -29, although Air Force reports do not.

In any case, on 2 September 1947 Boeing was given a contract calling for all studies, test results, drawings and a mock-up based on the Model 464-25 to be ready no later than 31 January 1948. This version was to have defensive armament reduced to one tail and two forward .50cal turrets, and an increase in bomb load to 12,000lb.

The inspection of the wooden mock-up was held as planned in January 1948, although, as mentioned earlier, Boeing's contract was cancelled at that time, and the Air Force expected to reissue the B-52 design directive to industry, taking the whole project back to 'square one' and quite possibly a new contractor. Convair in particular had been lobbying for another crack at the B-52 programme (Convair, Boeing and Martin had been the only airframe builders to respond to the original design directive). The mock-up consisted of one complete fuselage, empennage and right half of the wing, plus four additional nose mock-ups depicting various crew arrangements. The Air Force Board of Senior Officers politely stated that the mock-ups were useful, although their frustrations must have been evident.

In the meantime, the Northrop company had also contributed to the indecision over the Boeing contract. During the preceding year, the several Air Force commands concerned with new plane development had been considering John K. 'Jack' Northrop's all-wing strategic bomber. The all-wing (tailless) XB-35 was, like the B-36, a World War 2 design (actually, Northrop had been working on the flying wing concept since 1929 and had built several small craft so configured). The XB-35 first flew on 26 June 1946 powered with four Pratt & Whitney R-4360 Wasp Major engines of 2,500hp each. The turbojet version, of which nine were built, was the YB-49, fitted with eight Allison J35 engines of 4,000lb static thrust each. The YB-49 made its first flight on 21 October 1947. With an empty weight of only 90,000lb

Far left: The Boeing B-47 Stratojet landing at Lake Charles AFB, Louisiana early in 1953. Boeing led the industry into swept-wings and tailplanes in bomber design as speeds exceeded 600mph. *USAF*

Left: The jet-powered Northrop YB-49 Flying Wing of 1947 followed a propeller-driven version, the YB-35, and seemed to offer great load-carrying characteristics, but stability problems indicated a long and expensive development programme and the design was abandoned. *Northrop*

Below: A total of 385 Convair B-36s were built and equipped 33 SAC squadrons from mid-1948 until the B-52 replaced them in the late 1950s, the last B-36 being retired in 1959. *General Dynamics, Fort Worth Division*

and gross of 209,000lb, the 500mph YB-49 seemed to have a lot going for it. However, two YB-49s were lost in test, and in the end it was decided to scrap all the wings on the spot at the factory due, primarily, to political problems involving Consolidated and the B-36.

In the meantime, despite objections from Generals Craig, Partridge and LeMay, Air Force Secretary Symington, supported by Generals Vandenberg, Kenney and McNarney, decided to allow Boeing to proceed with the design of still another prop-jet version, the Model 464-35, which was to have a range of 8,000 miles and a 'sustained cruising speed . . . of 500mph at 35,000ft over 4,000 miles of enemy territory'. Take-off weight should be 300,000lb. This approval came in February 1948, but between March and October other changes were made which resulted in the Model 464-35-0, and as of 15 December 1948 the XB-52 prop-jet was defined as a 280,000lb aeroplane (Model 464-35-0) capable of transporting 10,000lb of bombs and 19,875gal of fuel for 6,000 nautical (6,909 statute) miles at a maximum speed of 446kts (513mph) at a 35,000ft altitude. A five-man crew had been decided upon, and armament would be in the tail only.

This 'Phase II' contract called for the expenditure of $29,418,373.00 and included construction of two aircraft, with delivery promised in February 1951. These monies were in addition to approximately $2,348,962.50 spent on the B-52 programme up to that time (had the cancellation of the Boeing contract not been rescinded in January 1948, the loss would have been about $4million because of funds not yet spent but obligated).

Such an expenditure would suggest a low priority programme today, but these were 1948 dollars, and spent during a time of very tough budgeting by the US Congress. Indeed, one of the reasons given for rescuing the Boeing contract was the anticipated reaction of Congress to a $4million waste of Air Force funds.

The Air Force generals were perhaps especially sensitive to such an issue at that time, because the USAF had just won its freedom from the US Army the previous September, and now, as a separate and co-equal branch of the US military for the first time in history, Air Force people were in total command of Air Force activities. Understandably, they were loath to suggest that they had bet $4million of the taxpayer's money on the wrong horse (power).

In May 1948 the Air Force asked Boeing to 'expand' the B-52 performance study to include installation of the new Westinghouse J40 turbojet engine. This pure jet version would incorporate a minimum of changes from the prop-jet aeroplane and would be equipped with external fuel tanks. Take-off weight was calculated at 280,000lb. This model was designated 464-40, and though it would have less range, the Air Force believed that the higher performance available in climb, ceiling and speed could justify the trade-off.

Further studies that summer indicated that as much as 4,000 miles could be added to the range of both the prop-jet and the pure jet versions by midair refuelling.

In-flight refuelling techniques were perfected soon after World War 2 ended, the first US aerial tankers being converted B-29s supplying B-50 bombers. This was an old idea, dating back at least to 1923 when the Army Air Service repeatedly refuelled a de Havilland DH-4B from a DH-4BM tanker, allowing the former to remain aloft for four days. The Boeing KC-97 tankers in service during the 1950s (and into the early 1960s) were essentially transport versions of the B-50 (engines, wings, tail and landing gears were interchangeable between the B-50 and C-97/KC-97). Again, the British were ahead of the US in perfecting in-flight refuelling, and the first KC-97s were equipped with English-made refuelling systems.

During the mid-1950s, the KB-50 aerial tanker appeared, which was a standard B-50 modified to carry some 7,000gal of fuel. The KC-97 remained the principal USAF tanker, however, until the KC-135 entered production in mid-1956. We may note in passing that Boeing got a lot of mileage out of this design (Model 367-80), because the KC-135 furnished its airframe to the C-135 transport and the Boeing 707 series airliners. Production of the KC-135B was halted early in 1965 after 732 of them and the earlier KC-135A were built.

Following the paper studies of the Model 464-40 version of the B-52, Models 464-46 and -47 were offered during the latter part of 1948. Then, late in the year, the Model 464-49 was worked-up on paper assuming installation of eight 10,000lb thrust Pratt & Whitney J57 turbojet engines, a powerplant then in its early stages of development, and the performance figures that came out of this study produced some wide smiles in the halls of the Pentagon. Here at last was a propulsion system of sufficient power to make possible the B-52 the Air Force had wanted from the beginning.

The Boeing engineering team responsible for this proposal was headed by Ed Wells, Engineering Vice President; Project Engineers Art Carlsen, Maynard Pennell, W.H. Withington, Vaughan Blumenthal (aerodynamics); and George Schairer. The aeroplane they offered greatly resembled a scaled-up version of the B-47 (which was well into its flight test programme). Its wings were swept-back 35 degrees; gross weight was estimated at 330,000lb; it would have a range of 8,000 miles, and a speed of more than 550mph at its bombing altitude of 45,000ft. Pilot and

Left: The B-52 wing underwent more than 8,000 hours of wind tunnel testing. *Boeing*

Below: Artist's sketch of proposed B-36F which, late in 1950, was offered by Consolidated Vultee as an alternative to the yet unborn B-52. By this time, however, the Boeing XB-52 had been firmed-up as a pure jet, while the B-36F proposal greatly resembled earlier prop-jet design studies of the B-52. *Aviation Week*

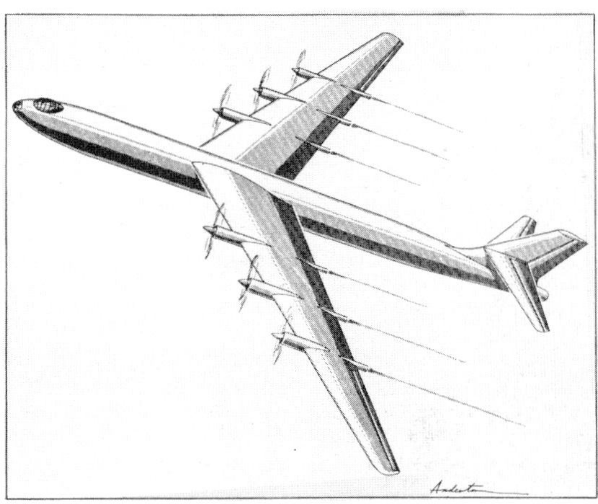

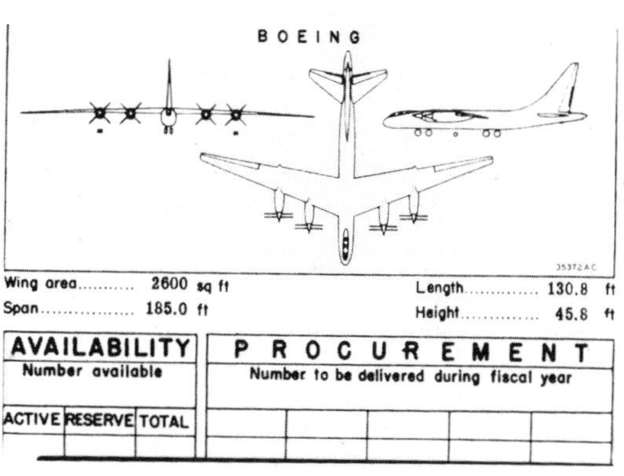

BOEING
Wing area .... 2600 sq ft
Span .... 185.0 ft
Length .... 130.8 ft
Height .... 45.8 ft
AVAILABILITY
Number available
ACTIVE RESERVE TOTAL
PROCUREMENT
Number to be delivered during fiscal year

Above: The original XB-52 proposal was for a turboprop-powered bomber as seen here in a Boeing drawing. *USAF*

co-pilot would be seated in tandem beneath an elongated blister atop the aeroplane's nose as in the B-47.

On 26 January 1949, after a meeting of the Board of Senior Officers, Headquarters USAF issued a directive authorising Boeing to continue the existing contract with conversion and development of the Model 464-49 turbojet aircraft.

Engineering refinements of the 464-49 eventually evolved into the 464-201 and the roll-out, on 29 November 1951, of the XB-52. The second of the two contracted prototypes, the YB-52, rolled out of Boeing's Seattle plant on 15 March 1952, and was the first to fly.

No official reason was given for the XB-52's tardiness in becoming airborne (it finally made its maiden flight on 2 October 1952), but old Boeing hands say today that it remained on the ground for all those months because some of its equipment was borrowed for installation in the YB-52.

The Air Force, however, had so much faith in their new bomber that Boeing was given a contract for 500 B-52s before either of the prototypes flew.

The YB-52 made its first flight with Lt-Col Guy M. Townsend in the co-pilot's seat and Boeing's B-52 Project Pilot 'Tex' Johnston in command. Tex lifted her off after a 5,000ft roll and an exuberant yell as she broke ground. He climbed slowly and remained in the Puget Sound area with the gear down, making gentle turns. After 40 minutes of this, with all gauges 'in the green' and the aeroplane handling nicely, Tex headed for Larson Air Force Base at Moses Lake in central Washington. They stayed aloft for almost three hours, an unusual length of time for the initial flight of a new plane, and after landing Tex had this comment: 'I am convinced that this is not only a good airplane, it is a hell of a good airplane.'

The B-52 test programme was undoubtedly the most rigorous to which any aircraft had been subjected up to that time. Delivery of the first B-52s to the Strategic Air Command (SAC) was more than three years away, and during that time Boeing's flight-test organisation contained more than 600 people. Test facilities were maintained at both Seattle and Larson AFB.

No B-52 was lost in test (the three B-52As built were added to the test programme in 1954), but there were some anxious moments. One landing was made with one set of main wheels retracted, and on another occasion one of the four main trucks jammed at its full 20-degree inclined position and 'rubberised' a significant portion of the lower fuselage in landing.

Static testing for structural fatigue and load limits was carried out on a B-52 airframe at Seattle beginning on 20 December 1953. A special concrete pad, stressed for a load of 85,000lb at any point and enveloped by 500 tons of steel superstructure, allowed every conceivable flight condition to be duplicated with hydraulic rams and measured by more than 3,000 strain gauges. Thus, simulated flight loads of up to one million pounds were achieved

Left: The YB-52 receives final inspection prior to its first flight on 15 April 1952. *Boeing*

Below left: The XB-52 made its first appearance on 29 November 1951 when it was rolled from the factory in darkness and covered with cloth for security reasons. *Boeing*

Below: Although the YB-52 rolled out after the XB-52, the YB was first to fly on 15 April 1952. Production models to follow switched to side-by-side seating for pilot and co-pilot and the B-47 type blister atop the nose disappeared. *USAF*

Above: The YB-52 was the first of the Stratofort prototypes to fly in April 1952 – here it is seen on that first flight from the Boeing plant at Seattle, Washington during which it stayed aloft for 2hr 15min. *USAF*

Right: The XB lifts off at Seattle during its initial test flight, 2 October 1952. *USAF*

Below right: 25 May 1952: the YB-52 at Seattle with its older brother, the B-47. *USAF*

Above far right: 49-231, the YB-52, stretches her wings during the period of increased flight testing in late 1952 and early 1953. *USAF*

Far right: Accompanied by an F-86 chase plane, the XB-52 began its flight test programme on 2 October 1952, almost five months after the YB-52 made its maiden flight. *Boeing*

– while the 185ft wing was deflected from its normal (no load) position as much as 10ft downward and 22ft upward at the tips.

These torture tests continued for two years until the Air Force was satisfied that there was nothing it did not know about the structural integrity of the B-52. Meanwhile, the wing underwent some 8,000 hours of wind tunnel tests.

The aircraft's operating systems, however, were a different matter. Later, in service, a depressing number of B-52s would be lost to systems failures. Actually, the first was lost in the winter of 1955. The second crashed early in 1956 when a turbo-alternator failure exploded a fuselage fuel cell. In mid-September an electrical fire in flight took another B-52 and all but two of its crew. Six crewmen and four instructors died in the crash of still another on 30 November 1956, and three additional aircraft were lost to in-flight fires during the following month. The B-52s were grounded twice during this period until new alternator power systems solved the problem.

If some of the new bomber's operating systems were less than perfect, others were very well conceived. The main landing gears, set in tandem, may be turned by the pilot 20 degrees to either side. The forward and aft trucks may be turned independently for ground manoeuvring, or may be synchronised to permit the aircraft to move crabwise for crosswind landings. After obtaining surface wind conditions, the pilot can turn the main trucks to the correct drift-angle prior to touch-down. The outrigger wheels on the outer wing panels (148ft apart) normally press against the ground only when the wing tanks are filled. (Prior to the G model's redesigned 'wet' wing, the B-52s had numerous individual fuel cells in each wing in addition to the external drop tanks.) On the main trucks, the hinges are so arranged that each truck retracts inwards, the port trucks go forward and the starboard trucks go aft.

The flight control system, aerodynamically boosted by anti-servo tabs, features rather small and relatively weak flipper ailerons sandwiched between the huge Fowler flaps. The ailerons are aided, however, by differential use of the spoilers. That is, the spoilers, arranged in seven sections on the wings' upper surfaces, may be independently activated. This unique spoiler control is also useful in balancing the asymmetric thrust resulting from the loss of an engine or two. Since the outboard engine pods, in particular, are mounted so far out on the wings, loss of power from one or more of these engines induces very powerful yaw forces.

The wings are mounted to the fuselage at a high degree of incidence, necessary with the double-truck landing gear and the level attitude of the aircraft in landing and take-off. Indeed, on take-off one had a sensation akin to that of ascending in an elevator as the ground falls away with the aircraft apparently in perfectly level flight.

Some elevator – accelerated by 140,000lb of thrust.

The P&W J57 engines fitted to the first B-52's produced approximately 10,000lb thrust each; but during the plane's eight years of production – August

Below left: The XB-52 rolled out of the Seattle plant on 29 November 1951 and here demonstrates its cross-wind landing gear feature. *Boeing*

Bottom left: A fully fuelled B-52 taxies on 23 February 1956 for take-off – note the drooping wings and the angled landing gear which could be turned to 'crab' the aircraft. *USAF*

Left: The 1,500gal external tanks were jettisonable prior to the G model. In background are B-52Bs delivered during the autumn 1956, with one C model at far right. *Boeing*

Below: This B-52G went to SAC in July 1958. The G had a cut-down vertical tail, a new 'wet wing', and smaller 700gal external tanks were fixed. *Boeing*

Right: The B-52F, this one blasting into the air with a pair of Hound Dogs, was the last Seattle-produced Stratofortress. Troublesome alternator problems of previous models were solved with the Fs. *Boeing*

Far right: Seattle-built B-52Cs. Delivery began in April 1956. *Boeing*

Below: A B-52C with flaps lowered to allow a B-17 to keep pace poses for a publicity photo. The C model, last to be produced exclusively at Seattle, had external tankage increased to 3,000gal. *Boeing via Peter M. Bowers*

1954 to September 1962 – power dramatically increased. Only 53 aircraft had been built by March 1956 when the B-52C appeared with P&W J57-P-29W engines rated at 12,800lb thrust each. The final installation came on the H model, which entered production in September 1960 fitted with P&W TF33-P-1 turbofan engines of 18,000lb thrust each.

During this period, gross weight went from 420,000lb for the B-52B to the B-52H's 490,000lb; and unrefuelled range went from 6,000 miles to 10,000 miles. Prior to installation of the turbofans water injection was essential to a take-off at full gross weight.

A great many other modifications accrued during – and after – the B-52 production run. More than a dozen bombing/navigation systems, of three distinct types, have been installed over the years, along with five different fire control systems. All did the same things, but with ever greater reliability and accuracy. The increased gross weights of the G and H models, possible because of more powerful engines, reflects an additional 60,000lb (10,000gal) of fuel capacity. All models have had defensive armament in the tail only, four .50cal machine guns up to the G model, and a six-barrel Gatling cannon of 20mm on the H model. The tail gunner was moved forward to join the rest of the crew beginning with the G model.

From the beginning, the tail stinger possessed both a special optical sight for manual firing and twin search and tracking radars. When the gunner was moved forward, closed circuit TV was added to maintain the gunner's view from the tail.

Perhaps the most controversial of the B-52's systems was the use of pneumatic power for operation of major accessories. Air, at 750°F and a pressure of 250lb/sq in, bled from the second spool of each engine, was piped through the aircraft to energise the hydraulics, electrics, air conditioning, water injection

and for de-icing. Problems with this plumbing, and the air turbines employed to turn the alternators, eventually led to installation of a more conventional system (beginning with the B-52G, aircraft number 359) in which shaft power from the engines directly drive alternators mounted in the nacelles and energise the hydraulics. This modification added some weight, but allowed elimination of most of the air ducting, clearing the way for the redesign of the wing and a greater fuel capacity. In any case, the direct-drive systems are much more reliable.

The most obvious mod, of course, was the shortened fin and rudder of the G and H models. A 20% reduction in area of the vertical tail was possible because of the success of the cross-wind landing gear.

Post-production modifications have made a truly modern global bomber of the B-52, and at a fraction of the cost of a replacement aircraft. Originally designed for a service life of 5,000 hours and costing the USAF $5,857,962 each, the modernisation programmes of the 1970s, costing roughly $4million per aircraft, not only added an estimated 7,000 airframe hours to the service lives of the D models remaining in service, but include offensive and defensive systems on the G and H models that exploit the most advanced technology in several fields. These programmes were:

1 'Quick Start', which involved the installation of cartridge starters on all eight engines of each B-52G and H. This allows simultaneous starting of all engines, and ensures that a substantial number of Stratoforts can become airborne before arrival of incoming submarine-launched missiles, the lower trajectories of which afford less warning time than ICBMs.

2 The Electro-optical Viewing System (EVS) involved some structural changes to house its sensors

beneath the aircraft's chin, a forward-looking infrared (FLIR), and a low light level television (LLLTV). The LLLTV provides a TV picture of ground scenes under conditions approaching total ambient darkness. FLIR can see through haze and even heavy cirrus clouds to give a good quality TV presentation any time of day. The sensors may be aimed laterally and vertically, and are coupled to the aircraft's bombing/navigation system, terrain avoidance radar, and flight director. Imagery secured by FLIR and LLLTV is displayed on 10in TV monitors located at pilot, co-pilot, navigator, and radar operator positions.

3 Phase 6 Electronic Counter Measures (ECM) was also installed in the 269 G and H models (which alone cost slightly over a million dollars per aircraft). The ECM package includes a deception jammer to counteract Russian pulse radars; an increased number of ALT-28 noise jammers; increased the number of infra-red deceiving flares; a re-worked station for the electronics warfare officer; and, externally, added a 40in tail extension along with two nose fairings and two tail fairings that house three microwave horns each. These horns form a 360-degree radiation pattern around the aircraft to further confound enemy radars.

4 The Short Range Attack Missile (SRAM) modification required re-positioned hard points in the aft bomb bay to accept the eight-missile rotary launcher (20 SRAMs are carried), plus two underwing pylons and the associated computer and other related hardware.

5 'Pacer Plank' was the $1.6 million-per-aircraft programme that added an estimated 7,000 flying hours to 80 carefully selected B-52Ds, and included what was, essentially, a new wing along with replacement of much of the fuselage skin. These D models are the so-called 'big belly' aircraft previously modified to carry internally an increased number of iron bombs. The capacity of each of these aircraft is 108 iron bombs, 24 of the 750lb varieties on external wing pylons, and 84 of the 500lb types in the bomb bays.

Entering the anxious 1980s, America's B-52 strategic strike force therefore maintains a limited conventional-bombing capability. Although the likelihood that these machines will ever be so employed is extremely small, the B-52Ds in service also have good potential as surveillance/reconnaissance craft. Meanwhile, SAC's B-52G and H nuclear carriers continue to represent one of the

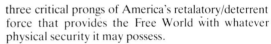

Far left: B-52H with FLIR and LLLTV installations beneath nose. *Boeing*

Above: 5 August 1954: the first production B-52, A model 52-001, lifts off at Boeing for its initial flight. *USAF*

Left and centre left: An early B-52B during operations out of Eglin AFB, Florida. *USAF*

Bottom left: This Stratofortress was in the last block of B models built after November 1955. The block lettering and white undersurfaces remained standard until the mid-1960s when camouflage paint began to be applied. 53-394 was the first B-52 to complete the round-the-world flight. *USAF*

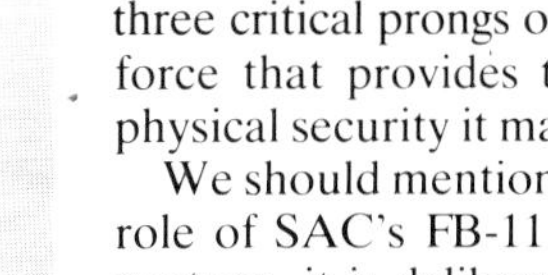

three critical prongs of America's retalatory/deterrent force that provides the Free World with whatever physical security it may possess.

We should mention that, if we appear to ignore the role of SAC's FB-111s in the Free World's defense posture, it is deliberate. The design of that airplane was so prostituted by the then US Secretary of Defense, one Robert McNamara, that this machine is neither fish nor fowl, and its primary function has seemed to be its enormous drain on Air Force funds. The US Navy, in whose name McNamara emascalated the original F-111 design (then called the TFX), had the good sense to take the position that the Navy preferred to do without rather than accept McNamara's brand. Your authors respectfully suggest that, if American SALT negotiators are determined to junk some US weaponry to please the Soviets, the FB-111s would be an ideal choice.

The B-52s that remain in service are, of course, equal to that ultimate, unthinkable mission should it be demanded. This has always been true. The earlier B-52 models – all now retired – were no less effective for their time.

The first production craft were three B-52As, the first of which made its maiden flight on 5 August 1954. The A models had a nose four feet longer than the

Above: The first B-52E, a Seattle-built machine. The E, which entered squadron service in November 1957, was the first B-52 to be equipped with the Hound Dog missile. *Boeing*

Right: B-52Gs of the 68th Bomb Wing at Seymour-Johnson AFB, North Carolina take part in the first 'Oil Burner' exercises on 2 February 1960. The B-52 was slated to take on the low level penetration of enemy airspace to avoid detection now that surface-to-air defences were becoming increasingly effective. Since the bomber's engines used a great deal more fuel at low level, the code name was quite appropriate. Later the standard low level training routes were renamed 'Oil Burner' routes. *USAF*

Below right: The B-52D started rolling out at Boeing in October 1956 and this model would go on to bear the brunt of BUFF operations in South-East Asia and then be rebuilt to see service up to the end of the century. *USAF*

Far right: Last B-25H Global Missile Launcher was rolled from final assembly at Boeing Wichita on 22 June 1962. Missiles at far right are the ill fated Skybolts that were cancelled in favour of the Hound Dog. *Boeing*

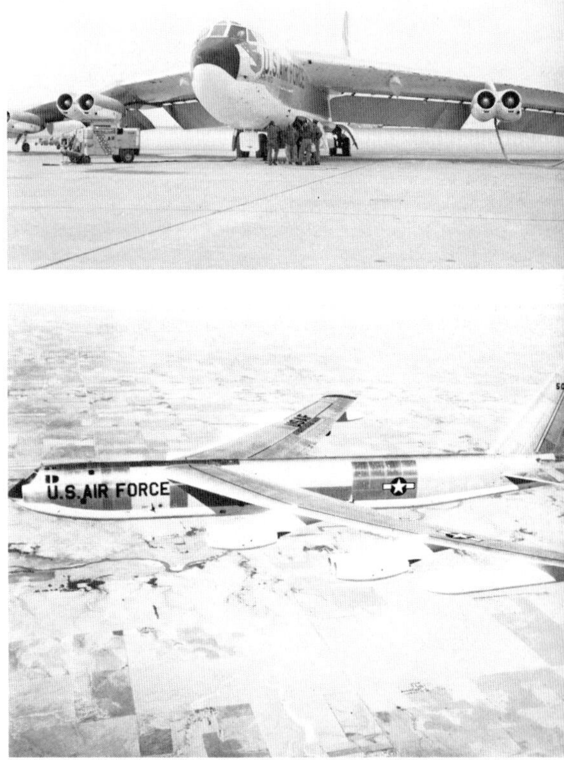

prototypes and a conventional cabin with side-by-side seating for pilot and co-pilot. These craft never entered operational service.

Fifty B-52Bs followed the A models, and the first of these was delivered to SAC's 93rd Bomb Wing, Castle AFB, California on 29 June 1955. The Bs possessed capabilities for conventional and nuclear weapons delivery and photographic reconnaissance.

After the B version came 35 B-52Cs, then the D, E, and F models followed in quantities of 170, 100 and 89 respectively, incorporating changes and growth reflecting advances in the state of the art. All, of course, were equipped with the 'flying boom' system for aerial refuelling to give them virtually unlimited range. The F version was equipped with J57-P-43W engines which would also power the B-52Gs.

The last models of the Stratofortress were the B-52G and H. In all, 193 G models and 102 H models were produced with the last delivery in October 1962.

Of the eight B-52 production models built, the A, B, and C versions were built at Boeing's Seattle, Washington facility, while D, E and F models were manufactured at both Seattle and Boeing Wichita. All G and H versions were produced at Wichita. In all, 744 were built – 467 at the Kansas facility.

By October 1955, as Boeing Wichita prepared to roll-out its first production B-52, more than 12,000,000 engineering man-hours had gone into this aeroplane. It is probably safe to say that an equal effort has since been expended on modifications and the development of advanced systems to maintain the B-52 as a powerful force for peace in the waning years of this century.

Peak B-52 strength in numbers of aircraft operational was reached in 1963 when there were 38 wings so equipped. At the beginning of the 1980s there are 18 B-52 wings containing a total of 350 Stratofortresses.

B-52 Production

Above: B-52 production ended at Boeing's Seattle facilities early in 1958. The two prototypes, along with the production models A to F were built at Seattle. Production continued at Wichita thgrough early 1961, where D to H models were built. *Boeing*

Left: The Stratofortress' tandem landing gear and wing mounted at a high angle of incidence results in take-offs that seem to suggest that the aircraft levitates rather than aviates. *Boeing*

Above right: B-52D production at Wichita. Note that main landing gear trucks rest in floor recesses. In the background can be seen new B-47s. *Boeing*

Right: Half the B-52's manufacturing time was devoted to fitting well over half a million rivets in each aircraft. The windscreens consist of 0.375in full-tempered glass, 0.34in vinyl and 0.187in semi-tempered glass with a Nesa conducting layer. *Boeing*

Far right: A B-52 skin panel that has been machine- milled to reduce weight receives a final dressing by hand *Boeing*

Above: B-52Es on the 'pre-flight line' at Seattle. Each machine was rolled out of the factory at a scheduled hour irrespective of its condition and the remaining work was completed outside. *Boeing*

Right: B-52 forward fuselage construction at the Boeing Seattle plant. Subcontractors provided 36.7% of each of the first 22 machines; 56.7% (by weight) of each Stratofortress came from other airframe builders by the time the E model appeared. *Boeing*

Above: The massive wing carry-through structure can be seen in this view as the front portion of the B-52 fuselage is mated to it. *Boeing*

Left: More than 20 subcontractors about the US built major sub-assemblies for the B-52. The horizontal stabiliser was furnished by Cessna; rear fuselage came from Fairchild. *Boeing*

SAC's Keenest Edge

The United States began the task of building a nuclear air strike force – with global capability – on 21 March 1946 with the formation of the US Strategic Air Command (SAC) under Gen George C. Kenney.

By the time Gen Kenney had established SAC headquarters at Andrews AFB, Maryland the following October, the five-year old B-36 programme had been revitalised, and the original B-52 specification had gone to industry in search of proposals.

Initially, Kenney was given 36,800 men, 18 active bases, and 600 aircraft, 250 of which were bombers – B-17s, B-29s, and B-25s – and the mandate to build a core of professional, highly trained people to establish SAC's peacetime deterrent mission and to develop and test new tactics and operational concepts.

During the next two years, as SAC grew to a force of 52,000 people and 1,000 aircraft, 'goodwill' training missions were flown to Europe, the polar regions were surveyed, and in between countless mock raids were made on cities in the US. Then, in October 1948, a new era began with the appointment of Gen Curtis E. LeMay as SAC commander.

LeMay did three things immediately. He moved SAC headquarters to Offutt AFB, Nebraska near the geographical centre of the US; he ordered the command to prepare itself for global operations, 'to be able to counterattack anywhere at anytime', and he personally saw to it that SAC personnel enjoyed the best food served by any military mess and that SAC families were comfortably quartered. He would demand a lot from them, and he would show them every suitable consideration in return.

True, this attitude smacked of elitism, a concept theoretically opposed to democratic principle, but LeMay believed that loyalty begets loyalty, that pride is a virtue, and morale all-important. All three factors must totally permeate SAC if it was to fulfil its mission as LeMay envisioned it. (LeMay's view of an effective deterrent force was one of unquestioned superiority, as opposed to the later and present US policies of 'sufficiency', 'parity', and 'equivalency' vis a vis Russia's offensive capability.)

Above: Gen Curtis E. LeMay was intimately involved with the B-52 programme from its inception; first as a member of the Aircraft & Weapons Board and then as commander of SAC. *USAF*

Above right: The XB-52 was the second Stratofortress prototype to fly. The leather jackets and wood-panelled Ford in the background date the picture to the early 1950s. *USAF*

Below right: New B-52Bs on the flight line at Castle AFB, California, 1 February 1956. *USAF*

Valuing skilled, dedicated manpower as his most critical resource, Gen LeMay founded NCO academies to improve the professionalism of enlisted men, and a lead crew school was established to act as a training ground for command-wide standardisation of tactics and procedures. He weeded out the foot-draggers and promoted the tigers. Eventually, LeMay's policy of awarding spot promotions for outstanding performance resulted in a high percentage of SAC personnel in possession of rank that was significantly higher than that enjoyed by other Air Force personnel with comparable time in service. But the SAC shoulder patch was worn with true pride, because it was well known that each individual proved himself in SAC or he did not stay. A 72-hour duty week was not unusual, and every man was expected to assume full responsibility for his

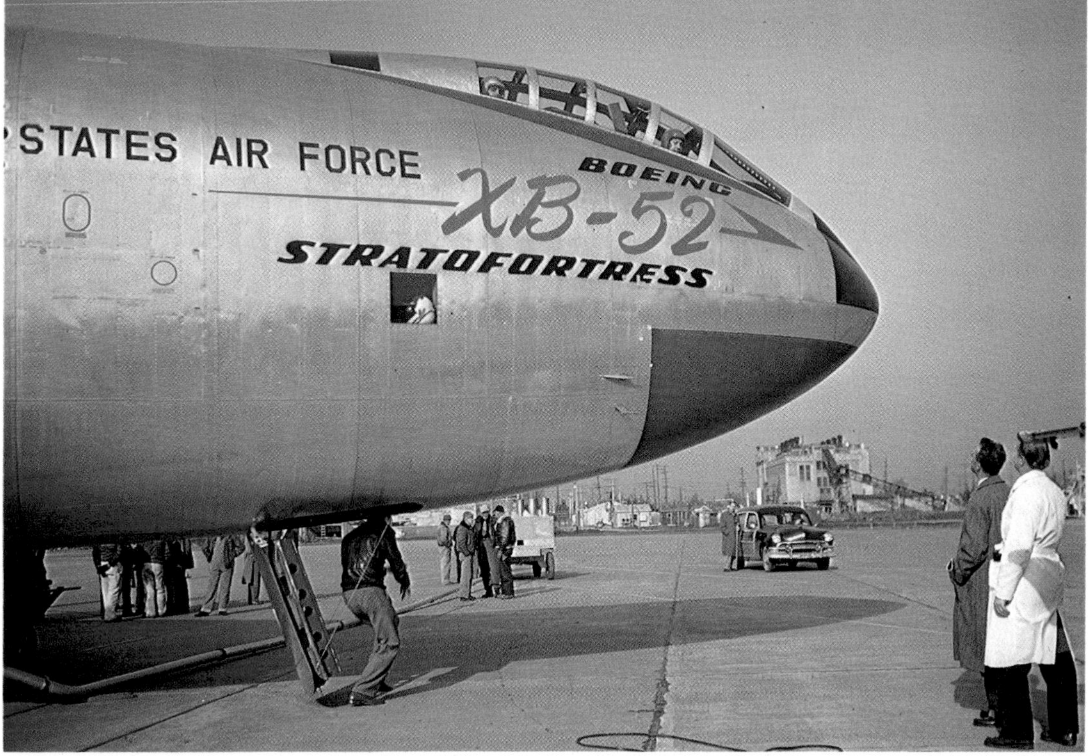
STATES AIR FORCE
BOEING
XB-52
STRATOFORTRESS

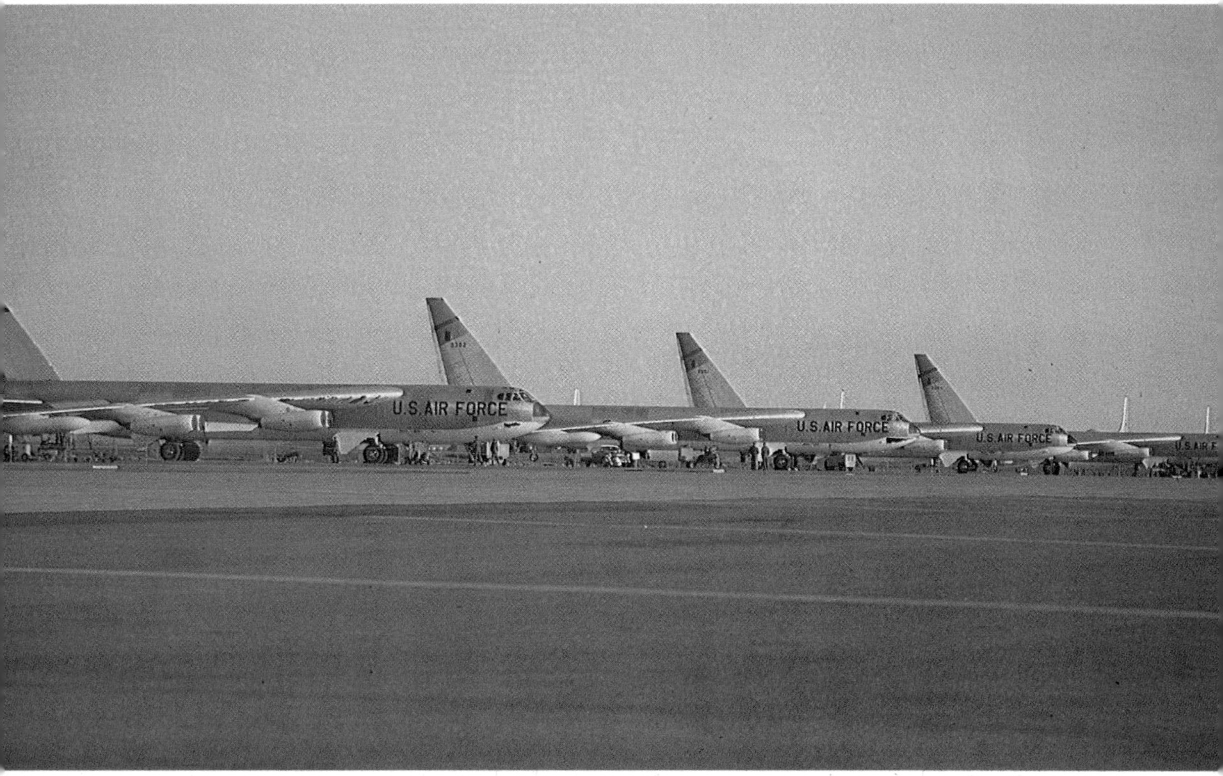
U.S. AIR FORCE
U.S. AIR FORCE
U.S. AIR FORCE

assigned task. No one passed the buck in 'Iron Butt' LeMay's command.

Thus, this bold innovator (who had sent unarmed B-29s over Japan at 7,000ft in darkness during World War 2 to fire-bomb that enemy's cities, theorising, correctly, that defensive anti-aircraft artillery would be set up for much greater altitudes) established the character of SAC for years to come.

When the Korean War broke out in the summer of 1950, SAC B-29s quickly destroyed all strategic industrial targets in North Korea and then, denied authority to strike at the true source of that aggression – Red China – served in a tactical role until the shooting stopped.

By the time the first B-52s were delivered to SAC in 1955, aerial refuelling methods had long since been perfected and were occurring at the rate of one hook-up every 15 minutes, night and day. SAC then contained 1,200 B-47s and a total of 3,000 assigned aircraft: B/RB-36s, RB-50s, KC-97s, KB-29s, C-124s, and F/RF-84s. Worldwide manoeuvres and overseas rotations were initiated to 'show the flag' and, by the end of the 1950s, a portion of the B-52 force was on a 15-minute ground alert while various dispersal concepts and an airborne alert were tested

as ways to insure a manned nuclear response to even the briefest warning of attack.

The airborne alert clearly guaranteed survival of some B-52s in the event of nuclear attack; but to keep a meaningful number armed and in the air around the clock for an extended period of time was deemed impractical because it seriously curtailed the training of new crews and other essential programmes while the demands on maintenance and support services were greatly multiplied. A 24-hour airborne alert was maintained during the Cuban missile crisis in 1962, and today could be activated at any time, although in recent years SAC B-52s relied on a 15-minute warning of incoming ICBMs – until the Soviet nuclear-equipped submarine fleet reduced SAC's reaction time. The 'Quick Start' programme, which allows all B-52 engines to be started simultaneously, resulted from that threat. Today, with crews in flight gear standing by 24 hours a day, SAC is confident that a large number of Stratofortresses (most observers estimate 120) would be airborne before any enemy missiles detonated on American soil.

Gen LeMay left SAC in 1957 to become Air Force Vice Chief of Staff (and Chief of Staff four years later). He was replaced by Gen Thomas S. Power, the man he had personally chosen nine years earlier to serve as his vice commander, and the build-up of America's missile force became Gen Power's duty.

The Strategic Air Command's first inter-continental ballistics missile (ICBM) became operational in 1959, and by the time General Power retired from SAC in 1964, the command contained 260,000 people, 2,000 aircraft, 875 ICBMs, and operated from 52 bases worldwide.

The following year, with Gen John D. Ryan in command, saw the beginning of B-52 operations over Vietnam and the accelerated phase-out of B-47s and KC-97s. The controversial FB-111 began replacing the supersonic B-58 Hustler medium bomber in 1969. The Minuteman III missile, with multiple warheads, was introduced into SAC inventory a year later.

By the mid-1970s, SAC manpower had been streamlined to a total of 144,000, serving at bases in the US, Guam, Spain, and England; and its effective weapons inventory included 400 B-52s, 70 FB-111s, 600 KC-135s, 450 Minuteman IIs, 550 Minuteman IIIs, and 54 Titan II ICBMs.

America's missile force remained stabilised (in number) at the end of the 1970s, but the twin forces of inflation and stupidity, the latter abetted by the

Left, top to bottom: Stratofortresses sitting alert at only a few minutes readiness, December 1958, Loring AFB, Maine. A major portion of SAC's deterrent capability was the mass launching of B-52s within minutes – note that the aircraft are fully fuelled as evidenced by the wingtip gear touching the ground. *USAF*

Right and below: When the Cuban missile crisis heated up in 1962, B-52s were placed on alert, fully armed and ready. These BUFFs are on airborne alert during the crisis, a practice that was later discontinued. *USAF*

HIGH SPEED BOOM
HIGH SPEED BOOM

Left: Boom operator's view of a B-52D fuel hookup during a deployment to the UK in May 1980. The aircraft belongs to the 22nd Bomb Wing based at March AFB, California. *Denis J. Calvert*

Above: A view of the cockpit during refuelling. The KC-135's director lights are visible as the pilot stays plugged in. *USAF*

Right: Detail of the B-52D Tail End Charlie gun position. *Stephen Wolf*

demagoguery of politics-as-usual, were steadily eroding America's manned bomber force, once the keenest edge of SAC's sword of deterrence, and certainly the most survivable in the event of nuclear attack.

The manned bomber, fully armed and with targets pre-planned, may be sent aloft without hesitation at the merest suspicion of danger, because it may be recalled if necessary for several hours afterwards. The ICBM, once fired, is irrevocably committed to complete its journey of destruction. Therefore, the firing of America's Minutemen must be delayed until there can be no possible doubt of nuclear attack, and many factors could introduce uncertainty, perhaps fatal uncertainty, not the least of them being the character and predisposition of the man in the White House whose hand hovered agonisingly over the Doomsday Button.

Meanwhile, it must be noted that the B-52s remaining in service are more effective than ever as a result of updated systems and improved weapons, and will remain highly important to the security of the Free World for the foreseeable future.

The first B-52s to go operational were the B models, built in Seattle, and delivered between June 1955 and February 1956. Squadron service began with the 93rd Bomb Wing at Castle AFB, California, while crew training was initiated with the 4017th Combat Crew Training Squadron at Castle.

Even as the B-52Bs were being delivered, production of the C model began at Seattle, and Boeing Wichita was at work on the B-52D, the first of 467 Stratofortresses (Ds to Hs) that would come from the Kansas facility.

About 40% of the B-52's airframe was subcontracted, and approximately 65% of the construction cost of each aircraft was shared by some 20 different companies. Cessna built the horizontal stabiliser; Goodyear supplied fuel cells, side panels, and wing stub structures; Aeronca provided the rudder, ailerons, elevators, and wheel-well doors; Fairchild constructed the outer wings, rear fuselage,

Above: A B-52B delivered in September 1954 touches down with wing spoilers and drag chute activated. *Boeing*

Left: The first B-52s to enter squadron service were B models built at Boeing's Seattle plant. A total of 50 were produced, 27 of which were recce versions. Photo shows a recce pack fitting into an RB-52. *Boeing*

Right: A B-52B with new reflective paint undersides but with the older smaller lettering on the forward fuselage. *USAF*

etc, and all mating components were bult to a maximum tolerance of 0.02in. Even the paint film thickness had to be carefully controlled because 275lb were added for every 0.005in of paint applied to the 185ft wings.

Actually, paint would prove to be a continuing headache for years. A primary reason for painting airplanes is that the aluminium and magnesium alloys used are highly susceptible to corrosion which, if not controlled, results in structural damage. Not until the late 1970s did the Air Force have a paint primer – developed by Lockheed – that was still effective after five years of test on B-52s. The savings promised with the use of this new epoxy primer were calculated in millions of dollars due to less structural repair and extended time between paint jobs.

The painting of B-52s, as well as all modifications, refurbishing, and major overhaul is carried out at the Boeing Wichita plant (co-located with McConnell AFB), and at the Air Materiel Centers at Tinker AFB, Oklahoma City, and Kelly AFB, San Antonio, Texas, with some engine overhaul being farmed-out, early in the programme, at least, to private contractors such as Pacific Airmotive. The original B-52 engines were good for only 500 hours between major overhaul; but today 4,000 hours between engine change is not unusual; and this is representative of the entire aircraft. Almost everything, it seems, has been improved, re-designed, or changed over the years, and except in general appearance, the late model B-52s still in service really are not much like those which entered service back in the mid-1950s.

If the modern B-52 greatly differs from early models, so does its tactics and place in America's defense posture. During the 1950s, the manned bomber was America's only weapon for mass retalitory nuclear action. Then, by the end of 1962, 126 Atlas ICBMs were in place at 11 sites, along with 20 Minutemen and the first Titans. Meanwhile, the US Navy's first Polaris-equipped submarines entered service with 22 of a planned total of 41 operational by mid-1964. US defence planners believed that this mix of missiles and manned bombers would greatly complicate Soviet plans to blunt a retaliatory attack by the United States.

That has been America's position ever since; and although all three of these nuclear delivery systems have been up-graded over the years, it is worth noting that successive US Governments since 1960 have allowed America's retaliatory/deterrent force to degrade, quantitively, compared to Russia's nuclear strike force, from a clear 10 to 1 position of superiority, first to one of 'parity', then 'equivalency', to 'sufficiency', and finally, at the end of the 1970s, a force that the Carter Administration described as being 'essentially equivalent' to that of the Soviets.

In any event, with no B-52 replacement planned, it appears that the Stratofort may well be the last global bomber possessed by the USAF, although it could well turn out to be the most significant military aircraft in history. If its mere presence in America's defensive arsenal should tip the balance in favour of peace during the next decade, we probably should never know that for certain. But Gen LeMay once pointed out that (*America is in Danger*; Funk & Wagnalls, 1968), since the US could not actually test its ICBMs against Russia, the true degree of their effectiveness could not be known. If fired in time, and if each warhead detonated on its programmed target, then America's transient 'essential equivalency' could indeed be proved (while at the same time having proved its failure as a deterrent). But there are two critical 'ifs' in that scenario – which is why the aging B-52 fleet continues to be an extremely valuable partner in the US nuclear deterrent triad.

Above: B-52Ds of the 7th Bomb Wing at their home base, Carswell AFB, Texas. This view illustrates the uppersurfaces' camouflage pattern adopted in conjunction with the black side/undersurfaces scheme. *Robert Löfberg*

Below: B-52D, s/n 55-0677, of the 20th Bomb Squadron/7th Bomb Wing from Carswell AFB, Texas, appropriately bearing the title *City of Forth Worth* during the SAC Bombing & Navigation Competition 'Giant Voice' in 1974. *Martin Horseman*

True, the Stratoforts have never tested Soviet defences, but the B-52 represents a much more flexible delivery system than the ICBM. If some of its avionics fail it may be hand-flown and its weapons eye-ball released; it is not irrevocably committed to a known trajectory or entry point. Flying at 400mph 400ft above the surface (normal training profile during the late 1970s), and with electronic countermeasures in operation, it should prove to be something other than an easy target for defensive weaponry that must seek to protect an area the size of the Soviet Union again missiles fired up to 100 miles from their targets.

As the B-52 fleet is armed with the cruise missile, the problems that will present to Russian defences will be substantially magnified – as witnessed by the Soviet's strident insistence that deployment of the ACLM will greatly jeopardise the SALT II agreements. However, as previously mentioned, if the B-52 is to continue to be a viable deterrent to nuclear war into the mid-1980s and beyond, it appears axiomatic that it must be armed with weapons of increased stand-off ranges.

This is not to say that the SRAM is not effective, only to suggest that, as Soviet defences continue to build, the B-52 will become more vulnerable and eventually must maintain its own survivability factor by reducing its exposure to those defences. In other words, it will need an air-launched missile of greater range.

Actually, except for its relatively short range, SRAM seems an almost ideal weapon for its purpose. Flying at three times the speed of sound, it is seldom airborne more than three minutes before reaching its target. Its 18in diameter gives it an extremely poor radar signature, and the fact that it may be launched in an almost infinite number of trajectories, with its carrier aircraft pointed in any direction (including 180 degrees away from the target), leaves the SRAM invulnerable to interception by any countermeasures currently known. Further, it requires almost no maintenance, has consistently shown in test that it will impact within 100ft of its target; and its inertial guidance system is so precise that B-52 crews routinely tie into it to navigate the carrier aircraft.

SRAM first became operational in 1972 with the 42nd Bomb Wing at Loring AFB, Maine, and at the end of the 1970s B-52 crews were still finding new ways to employ its systems. SAC crews say that by reprogramming SRAM's computer it could be used against attacking enemy aircraft. In the defence suppression role, SRAM can knock out enemy radars and surface-to-air missile sites to enable the carrier aircraft to penetrate to its primary target, which it can then attack either with its remaining SRAMs or with gravity bombs. The SRAM is powered with the Lockheed LPC-145 re-startable solid-propellant, two-pulse rocket engine.

An earlier nuke missile which armed the B-52 was the AGN-28B Houng Dog, carried in pairs, externally, throughout the 1960s and into the 1970s. The 1,200mph Hound Dog (no longer deployed, but in stand-by inventory) has a 500-mile range and is powered by a P&W J52 turbojet engine. It is 42.5ft in

Left: B-52G carrying SRAMs externally. This aircraft is typical of the Gs currently in service. *USAF*

Above right: 21 January 1961: the nation's first air-launched ballistic missile was to be the supersonic Skybolt, seen here beneath a B-52G over Kansas. It was still-born and never entered service. *USAF*

Right: Launch of a GAM-77 Hound Dog near Eglin AFB in 1962. *USAF*

Below: The AGN-28B Hound Dog's 7,500lb thrust engine gave this air-to-ground weapon a speed of 1,200mph and range of 500 miles. Two were carried. *Boeing*

Above left: As the aircraft get older, they get harder to maintain. Note the paint patches on this B-52G, s/n 59-2615. *USAF*

Left: B-52G recently engaged in the ALCM test programme with the Air Force Flight Test Center at Edwards AFB, California.
Stephen Wolf/Flightlines International

Above: 22nd Bomb Wing B-52D; just after take-off from March AFB, California and seen during undercarriage retraction sequence. *Frank B. Mormillo*

6695
U.S. AIR FORCE

Left: Wichita-built B-52D releases an ADM-20 Quail diversionary missile. *Boeing*

Above: The GAM-72 Quail, here in front of its mother ship, was a decoy missile built by McDonnell Aircraft. When launched from the B-52, the Quail gave off the same radar signature as the bomber – when several were launched, the missile was quite effective. *USAF*

length, 28in in diameter, and possesses an inertial guidance system.

The more accurate Skybolt missile, with similar range, was developed during the 1960s for the B-52 fleet and Britain's Vulcan bombers, but Skybolt was shot down by the incomprehensible defense policies of the Kennedy-Johnson Secretary of Defense, Robert McNamara.

The Subsonic Cruise Armed Missile (SCAD), officially, AGM-86A, is noteworthy, despite the fact that its development was discontinued in 1974, because much of the SCAD engineering and development effort was directly applicable to the ALCM. SCAD was an air-breathing decoy missile, with a radar signature indistinguishable from that of a B-52, capable of flight manoeuvres similar to those of its carrier aircraft, and could deliver a small nuclear warhead with acceptable accuracy. Its effective range was revealed only as 'several hundred miles'. SCAD's brief wings and flight control surfaces folded for launch from the SRAM internal rotary launcher.

Two principal types of gravity bombs are currently aboard the B-52s standing alert. These are the B-28 and B-61, the latter being a hydrogen device available in various yields, and small enough that it may be delivered by the FB-111. The larger B-28 is carried only by the B-52. Both weapons utilise parachute descent. A typical weapons mix for the B-52s on alert duty is four gravity bombs and six SRAMs, although this varies with target selection.

Approximately one-third of the B-52G and H fleet stands alert at any given time, and the D models, stationed at bases in the southern US, configured to deliver gravity bombs, may constitute a follow-on strike force.

Another piece of defensive weaponry long carried aboard B-52s is the ADM-20 Quail decoy vehicle. This tiny fibreglass jet may be air-launched from the bomb bay as a countermeasure. Its self-contained ECM gear creates a radar signature identical to that of a B-52, and carried in 'quick load' clip-in packages, multiple Quail releases degrade hostile air defence systems. In inventory since 1961, Quail had been largely superseded by more sophisticated hardware in the late 1970s.

During the B-52's early years of service, crew training emphasised high-altitude penetration and bombing techniques, but in recent years most training missions call for low level attacks. Today, a typical training mission includes the following major in-flight decision points from take-off to target:

1 Positive Control Turn-around Point. The point in a war situation at which the aircraft must have the 'go-code' order to proceed with the mission.

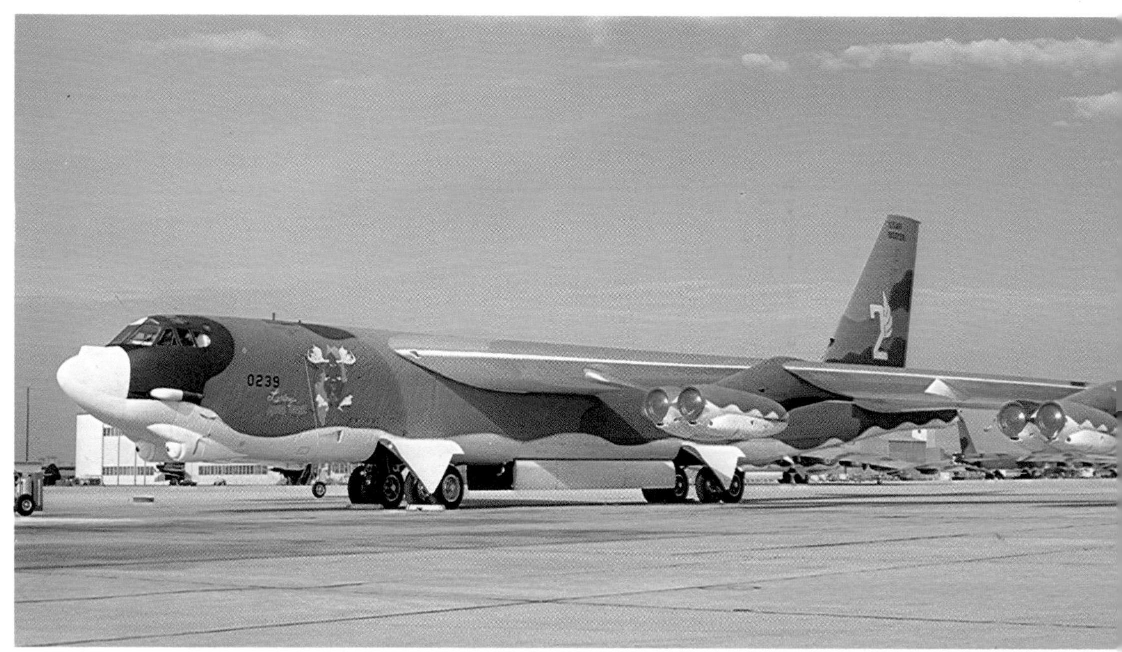
0239

Above left: B-52G, s/n 58-0239, of the 69th Bomb Squadron/42nd Bomb Wing from Loring AFB, Maine, at 'Giant Voice' in 1974; among the artwork additions for the event at Barksdale AFB, Louisiana, note the eyballs painted on the FLIR and LLTV pods below the cockpit and the *Loring Moose Gooser* title indicative of the low level profiles flown by the wing over the parts of New England.
Martin Horseman

Below left: Edwards, AFB, California, is the home of many unusual aircraft. This all-white B-52G was part of the stable of the USAF's Flight Test Center when the photograph as taken in 1975. *USAF*

Above: The 20th production B-52, a B model, delivered in mid-1955. All B-52Bs, along with some C and D models, originally began service with the 93rd Bomb Wing at Castle AFB, California. *Boeing*

2 Air Refuelling Initial Point. The point in time and place where the bombers on a strike mission rendezvous with their KC-135 tankers.
3 Weapons Release Check List. That point at which the aircraft commander, electronics warfare officer and radar navigator coordinate acts that prepare the nuclear weapons for release.
4 Primary Entry Control Point. That point at which each B-52 begins to descend to low level to avoid enemy radars.
5 Hypothetical Hour Control Line. A precise timing point en route to the target that must be reached within three minutes of the scheduled time. In a war situation, it would intersect a radius line around enemy territory.
6 Start Countermeasures Point. The point where the B-52s activate all electronic countermeasures.
7 Initial Point. World War 2 bomber crews will recognise this term. It is usually a known ground feature from which the axis of attack is plotted to the target.

As a means of giving co-pilots experience that allows promotion to pilot (aircraft commander) in as little as 18 months, two co-pilots are normally assigned to each training mission and alternate in the right-hand seat.

Average age of B-52 crew members in the late 1970s was below 30; average crew strength was about 1.5 qualified crews per aircraft, and the average crew member's experience level in B-52s was slightly below five years.

No weapons are carried on training missions, bomb and missile release accuracy being scored electronically; and each mission usually includes both primary and alternate release techniques to ensure that these professionals will, whatever the conditions, be prpared to locate and clobber their assigned targets. It is an exacting job, for which only the highly-motivated need apply. We will go along on a training mission in Chapter 6.

When the B-52 first entered squadron service in 1955, crew conversion required 10 weeks, although up to five months normally elapsed between B-36 operations and B-52 operations. Pilot transition was accelerated by the use of B-52 simulators (built by Curtiss-Wright).

All B-52Bs, along with some C and D models went to the 93rd Bomb Wing at Castle AFB, a bomb wing at that time containing three squadrons with a total of 45 aircraft (30 B-36s constituted a bomb wing). The 4017th Crew Training Squadron at Castle operated some B and C models. The next wing to receive B-52s was at Loring AFB, Maine, and it was initially equipped with C and D models.

By the time the first 100 Stratoforts had been delivered to SAC in autumn 1956, progressively ambitious training flights over North America culminated in Operation 'Quick Kick', record non-stop flights by eight B-52s of up to 17,000 miles. This was followed by a round the world flight in January 1957 by three B-52s. Five took-off from Castle AFB, but one landed in Newfoundland with engine trouble, and another, it was decided, should stop off in England to give RAF brass a look at the new Stratofortress.

An RAF team, headed by the Chief of the Air Staff, ACM Sir Dermot Boyle, and AM Sir Harry Broadhurst, AOC Bomber Command, thoroughly inspected this machine at Brize Norton, Oxon.

British reporters noted at the time that AM Broadhurst (a famed World War 2 air commander), limping as a result of having recently ejected from an RAF Vulcan bomber at 250ft altitude, displayed some interest in the B-52's automatic crew ejection seats – which were not guaranteed for more than 700ft upward ejection (pilot, co-pilot and ECM operator), and needed at least 1,000ft altitude for safe ejection downward (remaining crew on lower deck). Broadhurst agreed, however, that overall the Stratofortress was a 'magnificent' aircraft.

This particular aircraft was the third-from-last B model produced, s/n 53-395, had the name *City of Turlock* (Calif) painted on its nose, and was commanded by Maj Ben H. Clements of the 330th Bomb Squadron, 93rd Bomb Wing, a former B-17 pilot who had been stationed in England during World War 2.

The three aircraft that continued around the world were back in California after 45hr 19min, averaging 525mph for the 24,325 miles, which included four

Above left: Castle AFB, California on 1 February 1956: the first operational Stratoforts were delivered to the 93rd Bombardment Wing. These B models show a mixture of lettering styles on the forward fuselages and the aircraft on the left does not have the white undersides. *USAF*

Top: Trio of B-52Bs upon their return to March AFB after their record-breaking, globe-girdling circuit of 24,325 miles in 45hr 19min; 18 January 1957.*Boeing*

Above: The RB-52B recce aeroplane: the B models established a number of range and endurance records. On 18 January 1957 three of them flew around the world at an average speed of 452kts. External tanks had 1,000gal total capacity. *Boeing*

aerial refuelling contacts with KC-97s over the Atlantic, the Mediterranean, Saudi Arabia and the Philippines. The three Stratoforts, commanded by Maj-Gen Archie J. Old, 15th AF commander, landed within 80 seconds of each other.

Long distance B-52 flights became almost routine during the next five years. In November 1957 six B-52s flew a nonstop round trip between Plattsburgh AFB, NY and Buenos Aires, Argentina; and in December 1958 a Boeing Wichita crew remained aloft in a B-52G for 18 hours and 9,000 miles without refuelling. In January 1962 a B-52H of the 5th Bomb Wing, Minot AFB, North Dakota flew 12,519 miles nonstop from Kadena Air Base, Okinawa to Torrejon Air Base, Madrid in 21hr 52min to set or break 11 distance, course and speed records without refuelling.

There were other impressive flights during the B-52's first 10 years of service, and despite a number of systems failures and the loss of several aircraft, by 1964 SAC was judged the Air Force command with the lowest accident rate, 1.4 per 100,000 flying hours. After 10 years of service, the B-52 fleet averaged approximately 3,500 hours per airframe; and the fact that the first B-52 delivered, s/n 52-004, with 5,640 hours total flying time, was still operational (with the 7th Bomb Wing at Carswell AFB, Texas) was considered newsworthy.

Meanwhile, as we marvel at the longevity of the B-52 we cannot overlook a similar situation developing with the KC-135. A primary limiting factor on the US manned bomber fleet is the fact that it requires tanker support to be globally effective. SAC must maintain two KC-135s for every three

Above left: A B-52B of the 93rd Bomb Wing out of Castle AFB, California on 1 February 1956. *USAF*

Left: A B-52B is towed into the hangar for repairs at Castle AFB, California. *USAF*

Top: Stablemate to the B-52, the FB-111 is the only other bomber in the SAC inventory. Proposals have been made to re-engine the aircraft with the B-1's engines as the FB-111H to take the B-52's place but this has not met with much favour. *USAF*

Above: A SAC B-52H looks like this to the boom operator of a KC-135 tanker as the Stratofortress is refuelled. *Boeing*

Above: The first Wichita-built B-52D made its maiden flight 14 May 1956, and was delivered to Castle AFB on 26 June. It was essentially the same as the C model except for a few internal changes. *Boeing*

Above right: B-52Bs at Castle AFB, California in June 1955. *Boeing*

B-52s. In time of war the FB-111s need one-on-one tanker support. And since SAC tankers also have the responsibiity for the aerial refuelling of USAF tactical aircraft, the significance of an effective tanker fleet is obvious.

The tankers must be as dispersed and alert as the manned nuclear carriers or the whole concept of a manned global bomber force is clearly invalid.

The tanker support requirement is one reason the B-47 medium bombers could not remain in service alongside the B-52. That would have required a lot more tankers at a lot more bases worldwide. Once the B-52s were in place, a mere 80 B-58 Hustlers were deemed sufficient to replace more than 1,200 B-47s; and a like number of FB-111s would later take over the limited mission of the B-58s.

It is true that, officially, the FB-111s were said to have replaced early model B-52s that were retired; and had Secretary of Defense Robert McNamara remained in office all B-52s would have been junked and the only manned 'bombers' remaining would have been some 200 FB-111s. Of course, the FB-111 is not a strategic bomber, and SAC's proud emblem painted on its fuselage does not make it one. Gen LeMay characterised the FB-111 as a 'jury rigged . . . stop gap weapons system', although 'better than nothing'. Originally, the F-111 was conceived as a tactical fighter. McNamara insisted that the design be modified to serve both the Air Force and the Navy. The Navy refused the compromised result. Then, in an effort to justify his highly publicised 'cost effective' approach to the acquisition of defence weaponry,

McNamara decreed that the new fighter (which fell short of almost all of the original design specifications) be used both in the tactical and strategic roles by the USAF.

McNamara also closed a number of Air Force bases, cancelled the B-70 bomber project, and indicated that he did not believe in the manned bomber concept. It is therefore ironic that he was forced to call upon SAC and the B-52 to support his 'flexible response' theory of limited war in Vietnam. Gen LeMay, USAF Chief of Staff, who strongly disagreed with McNamara's theories and refused, as ordered by the Secretary, to keep quiet about it, was retired on 1 February 1965.

Earlier, the Defense Reorganization Act of 1958 had reaffirmed SAC's position as a specified command of the US Department of Defense, and defined the line of control from the President through the Secretary of Defense to the commander in chief of SAC, with the Joint Chiefs of Staff acting as 'executive agents' for the Defense Secretary. Although other reasons were offered, including increased efficiency, the underlying impetus for this act was the presumed need to firmly re-establish the principle of civilian control of the US military (undoubtedly influenced by Gen MacArthur's resistance to White House orders during the Korean War). This principle cannot be questioned; that is the way it must be – although inherent in its common sense application is the trust that no President or his Secretary of Defense will ignore the advice of the nation's best military minds.

In any event, America's three-pronged retaliatory/deterrent force survived the enervating 1960s and endured the malaise of the 1970s, while the flexibiity, survivabilty and reloadability of SAC's B-52s continued to provide substantive credibility to that force.

Future historians may well record that the B-52 was the most important military aircraft of its time – although we cannot guess now just when, exactly, was its time. Perhaps that is yet to come.

Vietnam

As early as the summer of 1950 the first US Air Force personnel were orderd to French Indochina in support and advisory positions on US loaned aircraft. The French needed help maintaining their C-47s, being used against the Viet Minh. By 1954, after the French defeat at Dien Bien Phu, North and South Vietnam had been formed after a cease fire, separated by a demilitarised zone (DMZ) at the 17th parallel. The Geneva Protocols did not require the withdrawal of the US Military Assistance Advisory Group, then authorised to have 342 men.

By September 1954 the South-East Asia Treaty Organisation (SEATO) was formed to lend American assistance to Cambodia, Laos and 'the free territory under the jurisdiction of the State of Vietnam' or the regime of Ngo Dinh Diem in South Vietnam. At the same time Ho Chi Minh announced his Democratic Republic of Vietnam in the North.

The commitment expressed by this treaty embodied President Dwight Eisenhower's acceptance of the 'domino theory' – if any more of Vietnam fell to the Communists, then all of South-East Asia was in danger of being overrun. The President decided to stand behind Saigon and its armed forces.

The French stayed on until 1957 to help train the small Vietnamese Air Force but the MAAG took command of the operation in early 1955. Armed struggle was not far behind and by 1959 the Viet Cong was active in penetrating the South through guerilla warfare. Eisenhower stepped up his aid in September 1960 by shipping 25 US Navy AD Skyraiders to replace the ageing VNAF F8F Bearcats . . . later 11 H-34 helicopters were added to this small force.

By the time John Kennedy took office in 1961, Nikita Khrushchev had committed himself to backing 'wars of national liberation', particularly in Vietnam and Algeria. Soviet aircraft became more than evident in their operations in South-East Asia and Kennedy determined to lend US help as a counterinsurgent behind South Vietnam. From that point on, the war in South-East Asia grew rapidly and American involvement kept pace with advisors, special units and several types of aircraft, including L-19s, T-28s, C-47s, B-26s, RF-101s, H-21s and C-123s.

From the very beginnings of the real war in 1961, tight controls were placed on just what US pilots could and could not do in combat. Kennedy wanted to avoid any military actions by Communist China or the Soviet Union. Those controls persisted and grew into volumes, lasting more than a decade with only a few lapses for short periods.

By 1965, in the face of the deteriorating South Vietnamese political and military situation, plagued by several changes in the country's leadership, President Lyndon Johnson committed the US to an ever escalating war to stop the Communist insurgents. Jet aircraft, such as the F-100, the F-104 and the B-57, were taking part in close air support of US Army and ARVN (Army of the Republic of South Vietnam) troops. The US Navy had committed its aircraft to battle as well.

The major USAF aircraft of the war in South-East Asia were also introduced to combat in 1965 – the F-105, the F-4 . . . and the B-52. America's primary nuclear deterrent, a high altitude-high speed bomber designed to deliver only a few nuclear devices, went through the South-East Asian conflict to gain the reputation of being the most feared weapon in the arsenal being thrown at the Communists. And, in many circles, the Stratofortress is considered the primary reason for the final end of US involvement in South-East Asia and for the end of the war at the peace tables. Few weapons could deliver the punch of the BUFF (Big Ugly Flying Fellow), as she became known to her crews.

'Arc Light', as Stratofortress operations throughout the war in Vietnam became known, began on 17 February 1965 when personnel from Barksdale AFB and Mather AFB deployed to Andersen AFB, Guam. The month before KC-135 tankers of the 4252nd Strategic Wing had been activated at Kadena Air Base, Okinawa to provide aerial refuelling for the Pacific Air Forces' fighter-bombers but their necessity for B-52 operations was a part of the plan.

Both wings of aircraft consisted entirely of B-52Fs, able to carry 51 750lb bombs, 27 internally and 24 externally. The only modification to the F models before their withdrawal from the theatre was to paint over the nuclear anti-blast white on the bottoms with black. This made them less visible from the ground.

Right: A B-52F releases its bombs over South Vietnam, August 1965, on targets selected in accordance with the US 'No Win' policy. *USAF*

By 18 June the BUFFs were ready to make their first strike. Twenty seven aircraft launched from Guam to hit Viet Cong bases in Binh Duong province north of Saigon. The crews and planners came away from the mission with some harsh lessons in their education of waging war with the Stratofort. As the aircraft were on the way in on their first aerial refuelling, two B-52s collided and broke apart in flames. Eight of the 12 crewmen aboard died.

Getting to the target, 750lb and 1,000lb bombs were released over a large area and the BUFFs returned home. In trying to assess results, little effective damage could be found, giving the press a field day on 'swatting flies with sledgehammers'.

Gen William C. Westmoreland, convinced of the aircraft's potential, came to its defence later by stating further evidence pointed to the mission's disruption of VC activity. It would simply take some time for Military Assistance Command, Vietnam (MACV) to use this new weapon effectively.

Part of the problem during the first months of combat was the processing of strike requests . . . they were given to SAC from MACV, then had to be approved by Commander-in-Chief, Pacific (CINCPAC) and finally the Joint Chiefs of Staff in Washington. Severe controls were placed on just what the B-52 was allowed to do and at times approval had to come from the White House itself. With the ever changing lines of battle, getting an effective strike launched could be close to impossible.

Regardless of the problems, the bombers began a series of missions which came to over 100 before the year's end and with ever improving results. The 7th, 454th and 320th Wings in turn relieved the force at Andersen as the wings rotated crews and aircraft from the States. Although saturation bombing of Viet Cong positions was the primary mission, by November the first direct ground support strikes were flown.

On 16 November 18 Stratoforts were quickly launched in support of the 1st Air Cavalry Division in the Ia Drang Valley as VC and North Vietnamese Army pressed in during a heavy counter-attack. 344 tons of bombs were dropped, the first of a total of 1,795 tons during 96 sorties.

The Marines asked for help in December as the Third Marine Amphibious Force was conducting Operation 'Harvest Moon' about 20 miles south of Da Nang. On 12 December Lt-Gen Lewis W. Walt watched the first B-52 strike from a helicopter, then wired SAC C-in-C Gen John D. Ryan: 'We are more than impressed with the results. We are delighted. The timing was precise, the bombing accurate and the overall effects awesome to behold . . . The enemy has abandoned his prepared positions and much of his

Top: Robert McNamara (left), Secretary of Defense under Presidents Kennedy and Johnson, and Deputy Secretary of Defense Cyrus Vance, two key figures who helped run Johnson's war in Vietnam, ignoring the advice of competent military leaders. *US Army*

Above: Tall tails at Andersen AFB, Guam in 1964. Note the 'O' in front of the first two aircraft serial numbers – this was a short lived USAF system to designate 'obsolete' aircraft – the first three bombers are B-52Bs. Shortly Guam would be receiving more B-52s for the initial build up for combat in South-East Asia. *USAF*

Right: 1966: The cockpit of a BUFF. *USAF*

equipment in great confusion, and this is making our part of the job easier.'

As the F models were introducing the BUFF to combat, SAC was already looking down the road to extended heavy bomber operations in South-East Asia. The entire B-52D fleet entered the 'Big Belly' modification programme in December 1965 to increase capacity to carry 750lb bombs from 27 to 42 internally or to carry 500lb bombs from 27 to 84 internally. The D model could still carry 24 500lb bombs or 750lb bombs externally. This put the maximum bomb load up to about 60,000lb, an awesome conventional punch. The B-52B was also phased out during 1965 . . . and the last KC-135 had been delivered at the beginning of the year. The entire B-52 operation hinged on bombers and tankers that were no longer being built. For that matter, Secretary of Defense Robert McNamara announced in December the phasing out of all B-58s and C, D, E and F model B-52s by the end of June 1971. Events would certainly prove otherwise for the Ds, now projected to last in the conventional role past the year 2000.

As 1966 brought increased B-52 activity, the D went operational in March with the 28th/484th Bomb Wing (Provisional), the primary mission remaining area bombing of VC base camps. The primary objective was to keep the enemy from building up large forces in their jungle sanctuaries. Nevertheless, 'Arc Light' went 'up North' for the first time on 12 and 26 April by hitting the Mu Gia Pass to slow NVA troops who were crossing over into Laos and then on down to the Ho Chi Minh trail.

Operation 'Birmingham' followed a few days later as B-52s flew 162 sorties, dropping 3,118 tons of anti-personnel bombs, to help the US 1st Infantry and 25th ARVN Division near the Cambodian border. VC defections increased as a result – the first two strikes alone destroyed 14 base camps, 435 buildings and huts, 1,267 tons of rice and a great deal more. By 9 May the operation constituted the largest for the Stratofort yet.

Enemy defectors were coming out of the jungles with stories of the terror involved when the B-52s hit without warning. There was simply no way to escape the immense destruction. Maj-Gen Stanley R. Larsen, commander of Army Field Force I in central

Vietnam, learned from VC prisoners that the raids denied the enemy use of some of their long held training and rest camps and communications and command facilities. A great deal of effort was being redirected into digging tunnels and other protective structures and to camouflaging unprotected equipment and facilities, not to mention almost constant motion and dispersing of forces.

By late June 1966, after one year in combat, the B-52s were dropping about 8,000 tons of bombs a month in all types of weather, day and night. The 3rd Air Division's 4133rd Bomb Wing at Guam was made up of about two B-52 wings, aircraft and crews, from the US on TDY (temporary duty) as of 1 February 1966. The normal tour was six months, until replaced by another crew coming in from the continental US (CONUS).

The major change in operations came in April 1966 when the 28th and 484th Bomb Wings deployed to Andersen with their modified B-52Ds, replacing the B-52Fs. By June SAC activated the 4258th Strategic Wing to supplement the 4252nd, flying their KC-135s out of U-Tapao Royal Thai Airbase, Thailand in support of the Stratoforts.

The B-52Ds were all the more effective when Combat Skyspot, ground-directed radar bombing, was added. 2nd Air Division Commander, Maj-Gen Joseph H. Moore, recalled that this allowed an accuracy improvement worth a great deal in spite of the restrictions from Washington placed on the B-52 force. The sites were mobile, adding to their flexibility.

By September Andersen had become an enormous beehive of activity. Eugene Perry, the Senior Master Sergeant who was shop chief for the 3960th Consolidated Aircraft Maintenance Squadron, recalled, after 391 working days: 'We have repaired 608 engines. We handle more engines in a month than most other bases work on in a year.' The BUFFs' J57s were pulled for inspection after about 1,200 hours of engine time . . . and at that point in the war the bombers were already logging 43,000 hours a month, which meant 60-65 engines each month.

A minimum of 250 man-hours were required to repair each engine during two 10-hour shifts run six days a week. The test cell was operational 24 hours a day, six days a week.

By 14 September the Stratoforts of the 3rd Division made their 5,000th sortie against Viet Cong targets, hitting a VC storage and supply area about 35 miles north of Pleiku. The mission was made by Capt Charles Elson's crew of the 28th Bomb Wing, Ellsworth AFB, South Dakota on TDY at Andersen, A. major portion of that total sortie credit had to remain with the early B-52F wings who had tested the waters

Above: Part of a three-ship cell at bombs away. These close formations were later spread out in trail to avoid mid-air collisions. *USAF*

Above right: Bombs away! Strings of 500-pounders fall out of this B-52D early in the South-East Asian Confiict. The results below were awe inspiring. *USAF*

Right: Part of the results of bombing by B-52s in the Tay Ninh Province, South Vietnam during Operation 'Junction City'. The BUFFs hit this area in War Zone C four times in one morning prior to the launching of US troops. *USAF*

since June 1965 – the 7th from Carswell AFB, Texas; the 320th from Mather AFB, California and the 454th from Columbus AFB, Mississippi.

In dropping 95,000 tons of bombs by that 5,000th sortie, the B-52s had also sucked up the major portion of the 100 million gallons of fuel delivered by the 'tanks' to the USAF units in South-East Asia. And this was only the beginning as more wings poured into the theatre. By December the bomb wings from Westover, March, Pease, Amarillo, Fairchild,

100

SECURITY POLICE
3960TH SPS
U.S. AIR FORCE 

U.S. AIR FORCE
USAF
70144

McCoy and Glasgow AFBs had come to Guam on TDY. If anything, the B-52 was becoming the weapon for the theatre and increasing demands were being placed upon her for more extensive use.

Gen Westmoreland later wrote: 'The B-52s were so valuable that I personally dealt with requests from field commanders, reviewed the targets, and normally allocated the available bomber resources on a daily basis.' He was always pushing for increased Stratofort sorties. In response to the demand, SAC placed six B-52s on constant alert at Andersen if the need arose for a rapid battlefield strike.

Demand was still too great to meet with the single base on Guam so in April 1967 a second B-52 base was set up on U-Tapao, Thailand under the control of the 4258th Strategic Wing. The advantages were immediately obvious. The BUFFs were only three to five hours away from their targets, requiring no aerial refuelling from the tanks – missions from Andersen were 12 hours long – and the sortie rates could be increased. By 6 May the 10,000th B-52 sortie had been flown.

Thomas C. Dorsey arrived at U-Tapao on 22 May when there were only seven B-52Ds on the field. Hardstands were still being poured and the living quarters were known as tent city. Bombs were offloaded from ships to amphibious Ducks, then taken to the beach to be transferred to the field. Later decent docks were built for this time consuming effort. Tom flew missions from both Andersen and U-Tapao and his memories remain vivid:

'We flew the living hell out of 'em. I'd like to have a nickel for every malfunction I had in combat but she flew real well and the D was perhaps the best of the bunch – it was modified so much they jacked up the oil caps and ran under a new airplane.

'The B-52D carried 104 500lb bombs internal and 12 on each MER rack or 47,500 pounds total. Our heaviest load was 104 bombs inside with 750-pounders on the outside – 64,000lb. We couldn't carry this load out of Guam due to drag, bad fuel efficiency and it was just too tight getting back to base. But out of U-Tapao and later Kadena this bigger load was used often. Every now and then we carried 750-pounders internally and 500-pounders on the MERs out of Guam.

'Gross take-off weight out of Guam was standardised at 450,000lb with engine start at 452,000 . . . the wing loading just wouldn't take any more. Once airborne we made a short hop north to Rota and then north-west to the islands north of Luzon where we made a turn to come in behind the tankers. 95-98% of our aerial refuellings were made on the way in over the South China Sea but there were two other routes – one over the Philippines, which was bad due to carrying live bombs over populated areas. The tankers flew out of Kadena, Okinawa, landed at Clark AB to refuel, then made their way to the refuelling track to wait for us.

'A standard on load of fuel from the 135s was 89,000lb and it was quite a feather in one's cap to get all 89,000 without a disconnect. It took 16½-17 minutes. We then flew to the mid-South China Sea and turned directly west toward South Vietnam to a common point, where we branched out to our pre-IP [initial point], IP and bomb run. There were three common exit points – north, mid and south of country – where we started a climb to 36,000 or more feet, even up to 45,000. Things got a bit touchy at this altitude since we were light, high and close to redline speed but the climb was necessary to avoid incoming flights. If we had been over the DMZ or above on "threat missions", as those over North Vietnam were called, we got double mission credit.

'The last common point was directly across the Philippines to 90 miles south-west of Guam where we descended out of 30,000ft for final approach. We normally had 30-35,000lb of fuel left and weather was carefully noted. Once off the target one of the first things we did was check our fuel state – if it was too close, we could divert to U-Tapao or Kadena and give the word on the strike report made by radio.

'This canned mission out of Guam ended up leaving us strapped to our aircraft for 13½ hours. Take-off was at 0400hrs and we chased daybreak all the way to Vietnam, getting back to Guam around 1600hrs. Total time, briefing to debriefing, ended up being around 15 hours. From U-Tapao missions averaged over three hours, from Kadena seven hours. Believe me, this was quite a difference and U-Tapao was always a great relief. Twelve hours of crew rest were given between sorties . . .on Guam that did not include briefing so we'd land at 1600hrs, begin crew rest at 1700hrs, then brief at 0500hrs.

Above left: A D model just airborne with a full load. The ground personnel at U-Tapao, Andersen and Kadena never received much publicity for their efforts but pride in the effort was usually easy to find. *USAF*

Left: The B-52F was the first model of the Stratofort to be committed to combat over South-East Asia. The first aircraft arrived in February 1965, from the 2nd and 320th Bombardment Wings, and were flying combat by June. This is 'Mekong Express' flying its 22nd mission in October 1965. By the time the F models left the theatre, this aircraft had flown 86 missions. *USAF*

About three of these spells is all you could take so crews were given other duties in their off hours which I considered unnecessary busy work.

'These other duties broke up crews . . . if one in the crew was sick, the whole crew stood down, normally in the Command Post at "Charlie Tower". I thought this ended up putting too many people there.

'There were also our share of thrills at Andersen. Runway 06/24 went uphill from west to east by about 80ft. It was horrendous . . . downhill for 5,000ft, then uphill and hit checkspeed (about 105kts). Once past this speed, you were committed to lift-off and I once lost an engine right after checkspeed going uphill. At the end of the runway there was a 500ft cliff that dropped off into the ocean. As soon as you cleared ground and the ILS equipment at the end, you had 500ft to play with and we often descended 300ft to gain speed . . . one guy went in, another slid off the runway with bombs sailing off. The Navy had to dive for weeks to get them all.

'Due to the almost continual rain, the runway was coated with algae and was slick as hell. When I was flying out of Andersen there were 94 spaces for the B-52s, not including tankers, transit aircraft or aircraft permanently based on the field. Stub 94 was at the extreme top end of the runway. If it contained an aircraft that had to be moved down to the centre row between the two runways, a tug could not hold back the aircraft on the downhill. This gave rise to another crew duty and I've seen Taxi Crews skid 180,000lb of aircraft downhill – nothing was more terrifying. We always used four engines, never eight.'

Tactics and policies for the B-52 often had to be worked through with some tragic results. On 7 July 1967 a mission was ordered to refine radar bombing techniques against a non-threat target. The day before Tom Dorsey had participated in a Skyspot mission to the South which was set up so that the aircraft dropped on time off the lead airplane. Confusion on the radio resulted as the release call was missed and the formation dropped late. The crew stood down for investigation.

3rd Air Division CO, Maj-Gen William J. Crumm, laid on the 7 July mission with himself in the lead of a tight formation. Dorsey was slated to be his number 3 man in the 'Finger tip' formation but his crew was down for rest and an inexperienced crew was put in his place. Dorsey and several of his BUFF drivers had severe reservations about the necessity of bombing in such tight formation since the situation was not like it was in World War 2 when mutual defence against fighters was paramount.

The formation used the lower gate into Vietnam, got to the pre-IP and formed up. At the IP a 90-

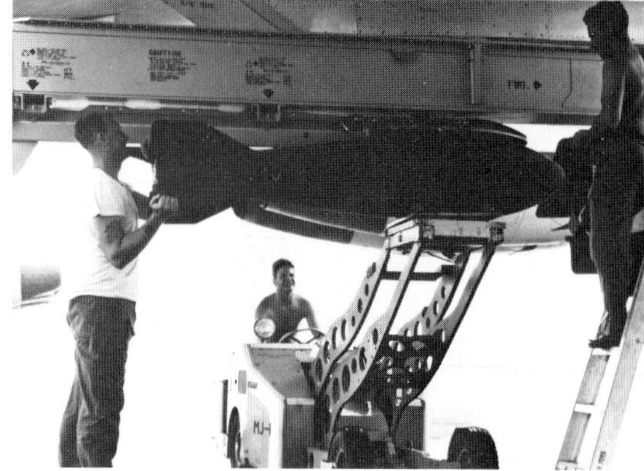

Top and above: 750lb bombs are loaded for the first Stratofort missions out of Andersen AFB, Guam, June 1965. The B-52Fs were loaded with 24 of these bombs on the external MER racks and another 27 could be carried in the bomb bay. 1,000-pounders could be carried as well. *USAF*

Above right: August 1965 – 750-pounders are being loaded on to a B-52F at Andersen AFB. Note that the fuses have not been installed in the noses yet. Rumours went around that many of the bombs were coming from World War II surplus stock but no one was ever able to substantiate this. *USAF*

Right: On 18 June 1965 the first Stratofort strike was launched from Andersen against suspected Viet Cong positions in South Vietnam. The first sorties were flown by a wing composed of personnel from Barksdale AFB and Mather AFB. The gear is just coming up and flaps are still in take-off position. Note the white nuclear anti-flash paint on the bottom of the aircraft. Later the aircraft were painted black on all undersurfaces. *USAF*

Below right: Early morning fusing and hanging of a B-52F's 750lb bombs on the No 1 MER. *USAF*

degree turn for the bomb run was initiated. The number 3 man allowed his aircraft to drift inside and he collided with Gen Crumm's aircraft – both B-52s went in and six men were killed, including the General. Tom feels to this day that had he been in that number 3 spot, with five years of fighter time behind him with a great deal of close formation work, the accident would never have happened . . . or if Crumm had not called for such a tight formation, the accident would have been avoided.

Proper formation tactics and methods underwent continual refinement during the first years of combat after tragedies such as the one involving Gen Crumm. The 'Finger Tip' formation was immediately dropped and the big gaggle formations were broken down into widely spaced three ship cells, with each cell stepped up in formation. On threat missions, 1,000ft separation was standardised.

On 8 July, the day after the formation tragedy, a B-52 pilot radioed in on the new HF emergency channel that his aircraft was suffering 'multiple malfunctions' near Da Nang, most of them electrical. The flaps would not come down but the landing gear did free fall into place – several engines were out.

The Command Post wanted him to land at Cam Ranh Bay but the pilot stayed with his decision to put down at Da Nang where the Viet Cong could fire at the aircraft as it was on final. This forced the pilot to maintain a higher approach altitude and he came in too fast, giving away 5,000ft of runway before touching down. The drogue chute was deployed but it tore off. The B-52 went off the north end of the runway and blew up. The gunner was the only survivor. The two accidents put the entire B-52 force into a long period of introspection and shock.

The routes out of U-Tapao were fairly rigid. Take-off was made to the south unless the monsoon conditions dictated otherwise. The bombers flew 70 miles south, then turned back to gain altitude coming 30 miles east of Bangkok and slanting up country to the North with 10 degree right turns every 10 or 15 minutes to angle across toward Vietnam. The return flight was on a direct line over the Vietnamese/ Laotian border 40 miles east of Bangkok to descend for a straight in landing on U-Tapao's runway 18/36. Routes were also flown south over Cambodia and some came back south after going north and vice versa, making a big circle. 45-50 missions a day were flown by the tankers to support the 30 sorties per day normally flown by the BUFFs from U-Tapao. Thirty six sorties a day was the normal number out of Guam.

Dorsey had the distinction of having the first SAM (surface-to-air missile) fired against a B-52 directed at his aircraft. The mission took place in September 1967, a threat mission six miles north of the DMZ, with bombing from 38,000ft. The briefing at Guam

Top left: Off from Guam for South Vietnam, a 4,400-mile round trip. The 12-hour plus missions were taxing and often boring – many pilots wondered about the tactical use in bombing several square miles of forest. B-52 effectiveness was not fully realised until later in the war although the Viet Cong greatly feared BUFF attacks. *USAF*

Centre left: Two B-52Fs en route to the target in early 1966. This type of close formation was later eliminated after some mid-air collisions. *USAF*

Bottom left: The 'tank' that got the BUFFs to their targets was the KC-135. Since the B-52s could not reach their targets unrefuelled, the 4252nd Strategic Wing was activated at Kadena Air Base, Okinawa to provide gas to both the B-52s and the increasing number of fighter-bomber missions into South, and later North, Vietnam. The tanker crews also flew long hours, staying on station between the Philippines and Vietnam for the Stratoforts. By June 1966 another tanker wing, the 4258th, was activated at U-Tapao Royal Thai Air Base, Thailand to keep the B-52s in the air.

Below: Bombs away, 56 miles north of Saigon, October 1965. Note the black paint applied over the anti-flash white. At altitude, this made the aircraft less visible, closely matching the colour of the sky. *USAF*

noted the possibility of SAMs with 35 miles range. Dorsey's three-shipper was stacked up 36-37-38,000ft 30 seconds from bombs away when the EWO (electronics warfare officer) called a SAM site 'up'. The mixer switch was flicked on . . . this would reveal the signal on the enemy radar as it locked onto the aircraft. Ten seconds went by as the screech of the enemy BGO radar found its target. Tom broke off the bomb run as the EWO called in the situation.

Flying off to the right, Tom pointed the BUFF toward the water, three or four minutes away, disregarding current tactical doctrine which called for a right break back across the initial track . . . the pilots had agreed among themselves that this was a good way to get hit. Five seconds after the break the missile went by, then a second – both exploded above the aircraft about 3,000ft away. The EW had tried to widen the band of the BGO-6 radar, inducing a false signal in the SAM, and it worked, allowing Dorsey's crew to bomb an alternate target.

On the way home Dorsey's crew talked among themselves about the encounter, knowing they would be heavily interrogated about doing things a bit different. Sure enough, the 3rd Division brass was out in force, from CO Lt-Gen Selmon Wells on down, to interrogate personally Dorsey and his crew. Tom recalls the incident with some reservations:

'The reason we were so heavily interrogated after the SAM firing was because somebody thought we had done something wrong (what, I don't know). My idea was to get out over water as soon as possible as a turn to the left would take us closer to Laos and the Ho Chi Minh Trail, which was alive with VC. If we were going to take a hit, I wanted to be picked up by the US Navy, not the enemy. At the time of the interrogation, the wheels did not know that we had not crossed back over track; they were just searching for something with which to hang us for having been shot at . . . We should have been decorated. I am very bitter about not having received the DFC for that action, when later they passed them out like cans of beer, and for things that were not nearly so critical. After all, we had just proved that the Tactical Doctrine worked.'

Even though 'Rolling Thunder', as the USAF bombing of North Vietnam was named from 1965 to 1968, used the B-52, most of the Stratofortresses' missions were directed toward the Viet Cong in the South, often in concert with Tactical Air Command's deployed fighters. Captured enemy commanders characterised the air support as disastrous for the VC. Meanwhile, at home, the B-52 was continuing to be phased out according to Secretary McNamara's 1964 and 1965 decisions. Both the D and E models were scheduled but the D's performance in South-East

Asia was rescuing it – the E and F, however, were being removed from the active inventory.

During the first three months of 1968 B-52 operations were stepped up in ever increasing numbers as the enemy launched the Tet offensive and pressd in hard on the Marine base at Khe Sanh. Around 30,000 North Vietnamese Army troops surrounded three Marine regiments and Vietnamese Ranger units, forcing Westmoreland to open Operation 'Niagara' on 14 January.

The monsoon set in, meaning that the fighter-bombers normally set aside for close air support would be unable to launch as many sorties . . . the only weapon able to put bombs on the target consistently would be the B-52. Enemy staging, assembly and storage areas were hit as well As gun positions no closer than 3,300yd around the small allied outpost.

Before too long it was obvious that the North Vietnamese were setting up bunkers in the buffer zone and the BUFFs were fragged to bomb within 1,700yd of the base perimeter. The American commander on the ground was a bit worried until he watched the strike walk all the way around his post, destroying everything in the buffer zone, without ever coming near his men. This was on 26 February.

The 3rd Air Division started 'Bugle Note' with Keh Sanh .. . a steady stream of six B-52s that hit the target every three hours with ground directed radar and continual readying of aircraft and crews at their bases. Targets could be changed as little as two hours before time over target, a great improvement for optimum tactical use. This method was so successful it was made a standard operating procedure (SOP).

B-52 operations in the theatre got bolstered by the *Pueblo* incident in January. The President deployed a great many more aircraft, including the BUFF, to South-East Asia in response to the seizure of that ship, and the Stratoforts began operating out of Kadena Air Base, Okinawa on combat missions. On 15 February Westmoreland requested the B-52 sortie rate be upped to 1,800 per month (compare this with 300 a month in late 1965) with the use of the Kadena-based aircraft. This rate remained in effect until 1969 when it was brought back to 1,600.

By April the seige of Khe Sanh came to a victorious end after the Stratoforts flew 461 missions, 2,707 sorties and dropped 75,631 tons of bombs from 14 January to 31 March. Later Westmoreland stated:

'The thing that broke their back basically was the fire of the B-52s . . . Khe Sanh is a battle that was won by you [he told SAC], and subsequently exploited by the 1st Air Cavalry Division of the US Army and the Marines. Without question the amount of firepower put on that piece of real estate exceeded anything that

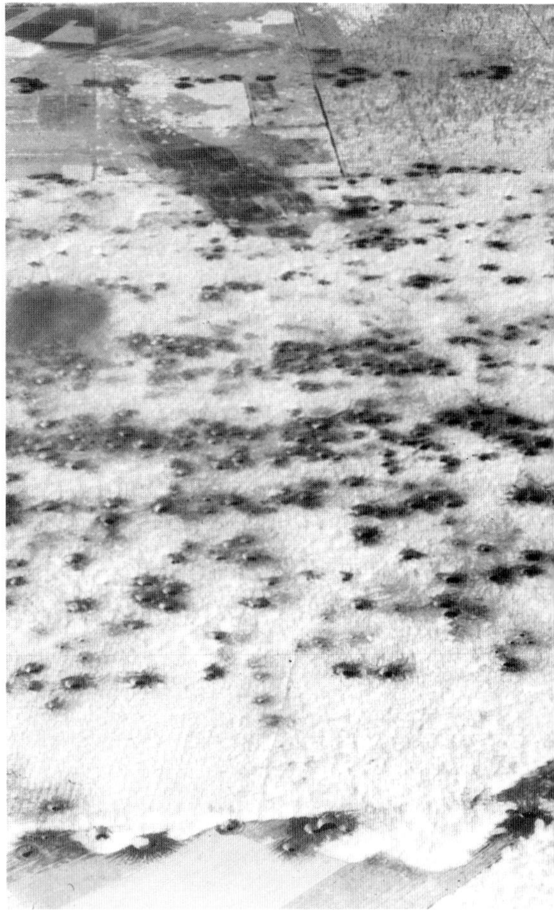

had been seen before in history by manyfold. And the enemy was hurt. His back was broken by airpower.'

Two Marine privates wrote a letter to SAC Commander Gen Joseph J. Nazzaro that reflects how most soldiers felt about the BUFF:

'We are Marines presently located at the embattled outpost of Con Thien near the DMZ. We would like to express our sincere gratitude and appreciation for the outstanding job your B-52 pilots and crew-members are accomplishing in this area. It is extremely difficult to express the feeling that comes over us when your B-52s drop their payload on the enemy positions around us. To us it is the greatest morale booster next to a letter from home.'

On 15 April 1968 the Stratofortress Replacement Training Unit (RTU) was set up within the 93rd Bomb Wing's 4017th Combat Crew Training Squadron at Castle AFB, California. The need for

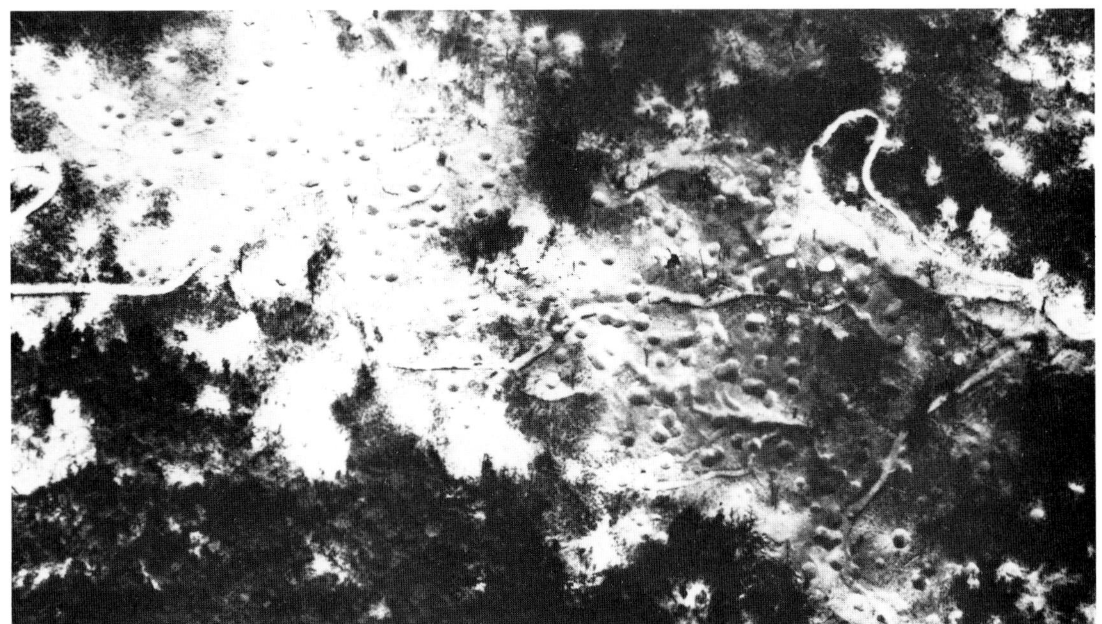

Left: Some of the early effects of saturation bombing in South Vietnam's 'Zone D', 1965. *USAF*

Above: On 27 April 1966 the BUFFs were sent against the Mu Gia Pass approaches to South Vietnam. This road, Route 15 from Vinh, led through the Pass to Laos and was a major source of Viet Cong supply. The utter devastation wrought had not only a direct effect on the VC materially – their morale suffered due to the lack of warning. *USAF*

qualified crews in South-East Asia was rising and the RTU's primary mission was to cross-train crews from B-52Fs through Hs into the B-52D. After two weeks of school, the crews were sent to U-Trapao, Andersen and Kadena. The idea was to get all of SAC rotating through the theatre.

As often as not, these newly trained crews moved to the combat zone in 'cattle car' KC-135s under Operation 'Young Tiger', whereupon they would be assigned a unit. After hours and hours across the Pacific sitting sideways in troop webbing seats, the tigers did not feel so young.

The sortie rate did not let up for the rest of the year as B-52s supported Operation 'Delaware' later in April against enemy bases in the A Shau valley near Laos, flying 726 sorties. Support of troops and interdiction was the major thrust in using the Stratoforts.

On 14 July the B-52s made their deepest penetration into North Vietnam 15 miles north of the DMZ when hitting troop and supply targets. The irony of the situation must have been frustrating to commanders and crews alike . . . the B-52 had the striking power of no other weapon and yet it was being sent only a few miles North while F-105s, F-4s and other tactical fighters were pushed up into the North on six different route packages to face incredible anti-aircraft defences. There is little doubt the Stratoforts could have been quite effective, as was later proven, but bombing controls were continually tight on use of the aircraft as fighter pilots tried to become bomber pilots.

On 18 July the B-52s were sent against SAM sites in North Vietnam for the first time . . . and this was primarily to help the fighters who were facing steep odds in trying to lay down enough ordnance to be effective bombers.

On 31 October 1968 President Johnson ordered an end to all air, naval and artillery bombardment of North Vietnam and 'Rolling Thunder' came to an end as of 0800hrs, 1 November. The idea was to de-escalate the war to move the North Vietnamese toward a final peace. The Air Force and the other services had flown around 304,000 tactical and 2,380 B-52 sorties, dropping 643,000 tons of bombs.

A vital part of all aerial operations in South-East Asia was played by the KC-135s which flew more than 79,640 sorties to refuel more than 330,090 aircraft from January 1965 to November 1968. The BUFFs, from June 1965, had dropped more than 886,490 tons of bombs while flying over 35,680 sorties. Yet this was but a preview of things to come.

'Arc Light' to 'Linebacker'

As the B-52 passed three years of combat in South-East Asia, tactics were set up in basically a non-threat environment. Flying in trail at least 1,500yd apart, the aircraft in a three-ship cell would be offset so that their bombs impacted a box on the ground 3,000m long and 1,000m wide. Several elements flying in trail would make up a wave and several waves formed a stream. Formation was maintained by the radar in the nose of each bomber.

The lead aircraft used its radar for navigation or bombing while those following dropped their bombs by timing after lead's release, or if they were out of formation or questioned the lead navigator's accuracy, they would choose their own release point with onboard radar.

Often the onboard radar failed and the mission was flown 'Bonus Deal', whereupon the tail gunner in the preceding BUFF would use his smaller defensive radar to guide the stricken aircraft directly behind, then time the drop on the leading aircraft's release. Since the offset was done away with, the bombs from both aircraft would land on the same spot, reducing the area covered.

The waves and streams all came in on the same heading with matching speeds and altitudes, then departed on the same heading outbound. Bomb bays were also opened one minute prior to release, greatly enlarging the BUFF's already large radar signature. In a non-threat environment this was of no great consequence but later, as the B-52s went up North into the heaviest anti-aircraft environment ever created, they would pay for this rigidity in tactics.

There were other tactics, such as turning on and testing the ECM gear a certain number of minutes prior to bomb release and the test dropping of chaff bundles, which announced to the enemy that a drop would be occurring at a certain time. As Dana Drenkowski, a 50-mission B-52 pilot who recalled these tactics for the authors, remembers, 'After watching American B-52 operations in South Vietnam and on the Ho Chi Minh Trail for six years, it may be assumed that the North Vietnamese became very familiar with American bomber operations.'*

Crews asked for a change in tactics, saying that if the B-52s were ever sent into the heavily defended areas their Little Friends were fighting for, heavy losses would be the only result. SAC staff saw no need at the time to change things.

In early January 1969 U-Tapao was converted from a forward operating base to a main operating base and the tents and small trailers gave way to the building of BOQs and permanent facilities.

*'Operation Linebacker II,' *Soldier of Fortune* Magazine; Boulder, 1977.

In February, the new MACV commander, Gen Creighton Abrams, made a request of President Richard Nixon to use B-52s in bombing enemy bases in Cambodia. The secret authorisation was made and from 18 March 1969 to 16 August 1973, the Stratofortresses flew 16,527 sorties, dropping 383,851 tons of bombs on VC, NVA and Khmer Rouge targets. Secrecy was initially maintained by announcing these targets as being within South Vietnam and all missions were flown at night under ground-radar direction. A year later, on 24 April 1970, Cambodia was invaded to hit the large concentrations of enemy troops and equipment and the BUFFs flew hundreds of strikes in support of the operation, now in the open.

In the summer of 1969 a B-52 accident occurred at U-Tapao after some confusion between the aircraft commander's airspeed indication and the co-pilot's. It resulted in an abort between S1 and S2 speeds and the aircraft hydroplaned off the runway with a full bomb load. In the confusion of exiting the aircraft, the gunner got separated and the rescue helicopter team assumed he was still aboard. On one of its passes over the burning bomber to drop fire retardant, the Kaman was caught in the final explosion and both aboard the helo were killed.

Above left: The early days at U-Tapao, Thailand or U-T. The 750s have been hung with care – and chalked with a few faces. Here the crew of Bill Turner preflights the bomb rack before boarding. The crews lived in tents and later trailers in Thailand until more permanent quarters could be built but missions were generally more popular since they lasted a maximum of five hours. *Bill Turner*

Left: As U-Tapao began to fill up with D models, the sight of several tails became the distinctive feature of the base. *USAF*

Above: The tanker force at U-Tapao in blast-proof revetments. The 135 crews found U-T less strenuous duty as well, not having to remain on station so long. These tanks served the entire USAF fleet in South-East Asia with prompt, often vital, results. Their sortie effectiveness was high and they were almost always on time for regular refuellings or for emergencies. *USAF*

Operation 'Good Look' was launched in 1970 after the B-52 sortie rate had been reduced for a year in the South. This effort was directed against enemy targets in northern Laos as NVA forces prepared for a major attack against outposts in and around the Plain of Jars. Tom Dorsey remembers being on the first mission, which began with a 0130 briefing:

'We ran five six-ship flights for 30 sorties as everything else stood down. Each aircraft took off with 4½ minutes spacing and going out was no problem but we needed adequate spacing on the way back to allow us to slow down for landing. A huge timing triangle over North Vietnam was "built" and it worked in spacing the aircraft.

'We worked 12 hour shifts – three days, three nights, three off. A crew of six also worked the Command Post with one in "Charlie Tower" on the runway for last minute decisions on problem aircraft.

'When we first came on there were several severe problems, such as a 21.00hrs brief for a 24.00hrs take-off. We had to rebuild this to an earlier 1900-2100hrs schedule. I flew as ABC (Airborne Commander) and overall mission commander in the lead. This was later deleted unless a threat mission was scheduled, allowing the lead aircraft to assume ABC. Normal speeds for threat and non-threat missions were 470kts and 430kts true airspeed respectively.

'The mission was successful, as evidenced by the lack of Communist offensive.'

Dorsey goes on to recall the problems at staff level: 'The thing that appalled me was the quality of staff people that we began to get starting about 1970. Many of them were staff weenies out of SAC HQ who had not seen a wing operation in years, and who were trying to stay out of the cockpit as FAC pilots in Nam, so they wangled tours at U-Tapao. Believe me, we had all we could do just to keep them busy doing things besides fooling around with an already smoothly operating machine – which U-Tapao was.'

As 1970 drew to a close, Andersen and Kadena were being phased out of the B-52 programme, generating only three and six sorties a day respectively. The entire operation was being centred around U-Tapao (although this would change as the war reheated later), where Tom was sent to open the SCAT in-theatre retraining programme to refresh the crews on the latest changes: 'It was a one day refresher in a ground school environment, followed by an over-the-shoulder mission given by an experienced crew. I got to meet a hell of a lot of nice guys over a period of five months that I had left to go on a six months TDY.'

Dorsey also was responsible for heading the team that rewrote the Combat Crew Manual in the winter of 1970-71. It had been set up for the operation at Guam with a small section in the rear for U-Tapao and Kadena and a great deal stuffed in the Combat Mission Folder piecemeal. All the non-deviation material was moved to the front, out of the CMF with Roy Lancaster's blessing. Much to everyone's amazement, it resulted in such a logical and useable manual, it was passed without any changes in spite of some 8th Air Force staffers who felt they should change some things just to do their job.

The BUFFs were now operating under the historical glow of the 8th Air Force, which had moved from the US to Guam as of 1 April, as the 3rd Air Division was inactivated. Certainly there was a strong tradition to follow.

In early 1971 the second series of missions were made into the Laotian panhandle to stop enemy troops and material from moving down the Ho Chi Minh Trail. From 8 February to 24 March the BUFFs flew 1,358 sorties to drop more than 32,000 tons of bombs. With the almost seven year record of accuracy behind them, the B-52s were given targets less than 1,000ft away from the ARVN units fighting on the ground.

Brig-Gen Phan Van Phu, commander of the ARVN 1st Infantry Division, made a point of drawing the NVA into a fight, then withdrawing just before the 'Arc Light' strike. He recalled that 'during the heavy fighting around Fire Support Base Lo Lo

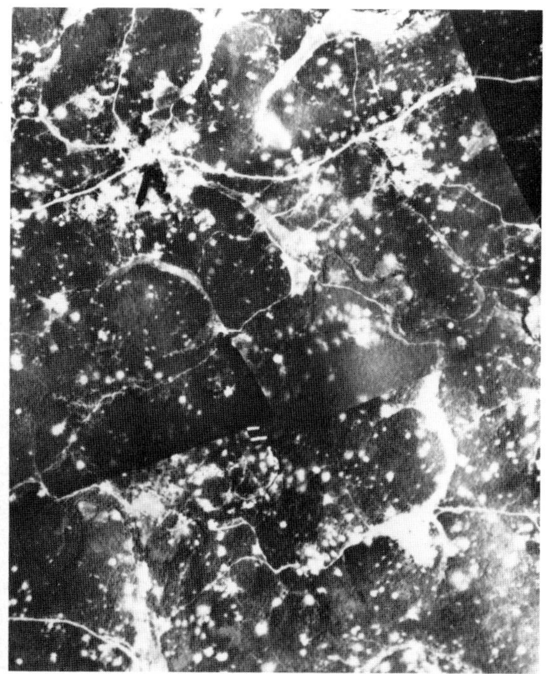

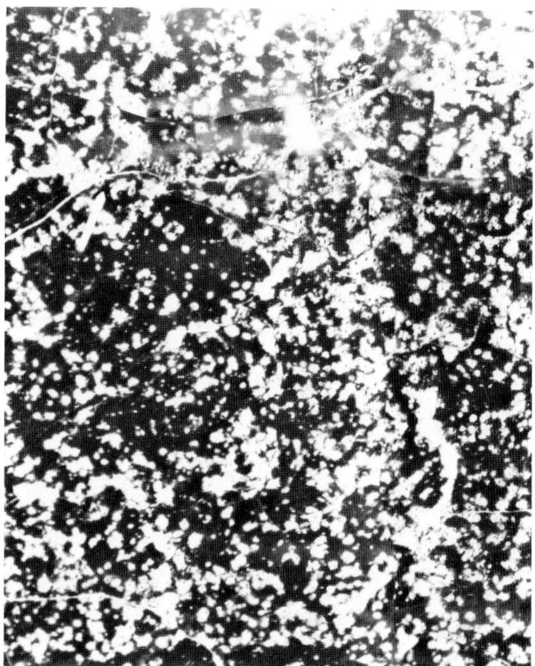

Above left and left: 18 October 1967: during and after a B-52 strike on Viet Cong staging areas in Tay Ninh Province, South Vietnam. *USAF*

Bottom left: Two months after the previous photos were taken, another strike in the same area – note the devastation in that amount of time. Crews wondered at times if 'clearing forests' was valuable but VC fear of the BUFF was intense. *USAF*

Above: Before and after in the DMZ. The saturation of several B-52 strikes is evident in this comparison of the same area. *USAF*

early in the week [late February], I called for B-52 strikes within 300yd of my unit. Many of the nearly 1,700 enemy soldiers reported killed in that fighting died in those strikes.'

The B-52 was continuing to be retired as all C and several F models were put in storage at Davis-Monthan AFB, Arizona, bringing the force to a total of 412 in the active inventory. In spite of its usefulness in South-East Asia, the total force was brought down to 42 flying 1,000 sorties a month.

By early 1972 there were strong indications that the North Vietnamese were going to launch a major offensive – troops and material were coming down the Ho Chi Minh Trail in ever increasing numbers. MACV asked for heavy B-52 strikes to stop the potential assault and on 8 February the BUFF sortie rate was upped to 1,200 per day with expansion to 1,500 a day. All over the US B-52 wings were being notified of the need for aircraft and crews as 'Bullet Shot', the new name for the Stratofort buildup, got under way.

In April and May three more deployments brought the total number of B-52s up to 200 (as compared with 130 during previous peak activity in the theatre) and 3,150 sorties a month. Andersen on Guam was hopping again as tents sprang up to accommodate the aircraft – and this time there were more aircraft than there were parking spots, which meant 30 aircraft had to be in the air at all times. Personnel on TDY continued to swell to over 4,000 in 'Canvas Court' and health conditions suffered as a result – no hot water, overflowing toilets and asthma from mouldy mattresses. Andersen physician William Obenour made the conditions known and was promptly transferred home to Carswell AFB by Andersen officials who denied his statements.

Newer B-52Gs were the major portion of 'Bullet Shot' deployments, modified to carry larger payloads and carrying enough fuel to eliminate the need for aerial refuelling on many missions. They would not soldier on with the B-52Ds as the war heated up.

In late March the North Vietnamese finally launched their offensive against Quang Tri City, Kontum and An Loc as three divisions moved across the DMZ with one victory after the other. The BUFFs flew 132 sorties to stem the tide but all of April saw a continual movement of the enemy south. On 9 April one B-52 was hit by a SAM but made it down at Da Nang.

Robert Johnson was a part of the B-52D section of 'Bullet Shot', coming to Andersen TDY from Westover AFB in March as a flight line maintenance officer. Bob recalls:

'We launched 55-100, now on display at Andersen as the Arc Light Memorial, from Westover on a flight to Kelly AFB for overhaul. During the flight, our unit, the 99th Bomb Wing, received a message to launch all Ds (16 aircraft) and supporting 135s to Guam. 5100 diverted to Guam. It was badly in need of a paint job and the gloss black had peeled much like a house. This aircraft consistently launched and flew with a minimum of OMS [operational maintenance] and FMS [field maintenance] work, but many crews wrote all eight engines up for excessive fuel consumption. The corrective action in the 781s [maintenance handbook] was always "needs a paint job".

'The majority of the 1972 missions were flown on a fairly rigid launch schedule. Twenty-two cells of aircraft (three per cell) were launched a day. For every cell or "Ballgame" as they were referred to by job control, five tail numbers were assigned. Three primary aircraft would start engines approximately 45 minutes prior to launch. The primary spare was pre-flighted and a full aircrew had the aircraft readied with engines running and all systems operational. The secondary spare was pre-flighted only. All aircraft carried a standard load of 42 750s internal and 24 500s external. If any uncorrectable mechanical difficulties occurred with any of the primary aircraft, the aircrew from that bird "Bagdragged" to the primary spare and the spare crew was taken to the secondary spare. All in all, a real hustle!'

Johnson, as a maintenance officer, always wondered 'why the U-Tapao operation used pre-loads of 750s for the bomb bay [in big belly clips] and the Guam operation always used individual loading. The 750s at U-T were loaded in bomb racks and transported to the flightline on trailers at which point they were raised into the bomb bay . . .'

Kadena on Okinawa came back into action in support of the deployments by providing KC-135 support but when the island reverted to Japanese control on 15 May, anti-war protestors made sure B-52s would be kept from operating out of the island. When several BUFFs had to divert to Kadena due to weather at Guam, the protestors made their displeasure known and the base was not used by the bombers except in extreme emergency.

By mid-year KC-135s were operating not only from U-Tapao and Kadena, but from Clark AB, Philippines and Don Muang, Korat and Takhli in Thailand in support of what became known as 'Linebacker', which lasted from May to October 1972 The focal point of the operation was the two rail networks that fed Hanoi from China, carrying supportive material to the North's offensive. The first strike back into the North by the B-52s was made on 9 April 1972 as the bombers continued to hit targets in the invaded areas of South Vietnam. The NVA invasion was finally turned back and by 26 June major enemy forces had withdrawn from An Loc but the war up North was just getting under way.

On the 9 April mission 12 Stratoforts hit POL storage tanks and a rail yard at Vinh; one B-52 was hit by a SAM, losing its left outboard fuel tank and getting riddled in the process. It got down at Da Nang. Three days later 18 B-52s struck Bai Thuong airfield and chewed up the runway and taxiways along with destroying a MiG-17 and four AA sites.

Haiphong POL storage bases were hit on 15 April by 17 BUFFs . . . the crews counted 35 SAMs launched but all missed. The bomber crews were finally getting up North where their Little Friend fighter crews had been fighting a tremendous battle. Nixon was gambling with his major weapon system and the outcry from Hanoi was heard round the world.

SAM activity became more and more evident. On 21 and 23 April 25 SAMs were fired each day at the B-52s as they hit targets in the Thanh Hoa area. One bomber was hit but made it into Da Nang with no crew losses. Damage from these strikes of only 18 aircraft each, was quite evident.

Vincent Osborne was an EWO during that period. He recalled what it was like to go out and fly.

'To load the aircraft and preflight took 45 minutes. There was not enough air conditioning in the aircraft and the ramp heated up greatly so we'd normally take a 10-minute break before engine start to get the sweat out of our flight suits – they were Nomex so the sweat would not evaporate through the fabric. The D model had to be 140 degrees inside the EW's compartment but this wasn't unbearable up to 1972 when we wore the K3B suit which soaked up the sweat and let it evaporate. The Nomex could stay wet for half the mission and one went from burning up to freezing. I really needed that short break to get the sweat out.

'Chasing the sunset out of Guam for four hours was just beautiful but the missions were 12 hours long. Out of U-Tapao we didn't have to carry as much gear, just a light jacket. If the cabin air conditioning failed, we could get down before getting too cold. From Guam we always carried heavy winter gear.

'From U-Tapao to the target was normally an hour, then home and crew recovery was quick as well. For every 20 missions the Air Medal was awarded – double credit missions over the North could bring that down to 10 missions for one. If there was heavy action, then a medal was awarded if one bothered to put in for it.

'Combat pay was $65 a month for hostile fire TDY with a family separation allowance of $1 per day for officers. This did not offset the hardships on family life. Infidelity was a major problem and those waiting at home were faced with things they could not handle. There were many divorces.

'Most of us felt we were doing a good job for the good guys on the ground. Our bombing was accurate but we only made the news for hitting the wrong target. The guys felt the job was worth the personal sacrifice at the time.

'The standard BUFF joke at the time went something lik this . . . an F-4 came by a B-52 and did a few aileron rolls while radioing, "Bet you can't do that!" The 52's response was, "OK, see if you can do this." After a pause the 52 radioed back, "Did you see that?" The F-4 replied, "See what?" "We just shut down two engines".'

Robert P. Jacober, Jr recalled upgrading to combat ready status by getting 10 orientation flights.

'The pilots were run in and out of the left seat, particularly on the five to eight minute downwind leg for landing. We would buckle and unbuckle all the time so that the Instructor Pilot just stayed in the right seat. The idea was that if one can land from the left seat, one can land from the right and all the co-pilots would log this left seat time as Aircraft Commander rather than "Co". I think this time helped me upgrade to Aircraft Commander, the first in SAC to do so, faster than I would have otherwise. When I first got in I was told I would have to be a captain with 2,000 hours before upgrading but I ended up with 1,100 hours total and 750 in the aircraft when it happened.

'We flew all of our missions at combat heavyweight limits – at S2 or unstick speed we were just passing over the cliff at Guam and trying for the flap speed of 180kts. To get a climb speed of 280kts took five to 15 minutes at times! If we were light and had water injection, the aircraft got up rapidly.

Below: Up and out of Andersen AFB, Guam to chase the sunset. Heading west for so long, the BUFF crews were treated to one continuous sunset for several hours – but glare often became a problem that was never completely solved. *USAF*

50087

'One crew had a skillet hooked up so that they could cook up breakfast or dinner on the way out and back in. The missions were so long we usually took turns sleeping on the way back or on the way in. Coming back a slight turn was made at the Philippines and once, after fighting sleep, I responded to Nav's turn command by turning the auto-pilot knob and falling asleep. The B-52 turned 60deg or 70deg instead of 5 or 10. The Nav queried me a couple times, then screamed to wake me up! We just got plain tired due to the nature of the beast.

'Due to the length of the missions in the Gs, there was no aerial refuelling or landing practice for the co-pilot. In six months, the Cos would lose proficiency so we started to take on token amounts of fuel from the tankers for practice.

'When the fuel totaliser hit 20,000lb, the B-52 was supposed to be on the deck with engines shut down due to erratic readings. 15,000lb was the absolute limit. I came into Guam once very low on fuel after a mission. The weather was bad and I made one missed approach. On the go-around there was only enough fuel for one approach, then we'd have to eject. With a radar altimeter aboard the procedure we decided upon was to stay on the numbers, get to decision height [lowest allowable approach altitude], then go below that. The Pilot would fly the instrument approach then I would take over when I had visual sight of the ground – this procedure was not standard then, but it is used often now.

'As we came down I saw a flash of white below the minimum altitude and called, "I've got the airplane!" I had picked up the white coral dirt road at the end of the runway extension and followed it until it ran out . . . then the strobes came into sight at the end of the runway. I landed long and made it.'

There seemed to be no doubt about the opinions of those flying from Guam . . . they would much rather be at U-Tapao with Pattea Beach and the lovely people from the 'land of smiles'. Jacober was given the following 'Official Statement' upon leaving the island

Date: Day................. Month........... Year..........
I................swear that while exiled to Guam, also known as The Rock, Land of the POGs, AMOGs, and other unmentional names, I swear that I was not tortured. I also can say that I was not threatened to sign this typed statement. I was treated as an equal and was fed like the rest, twice a week. I was given my mail as it came, untouched and unopened except to censor any obscene words and eliminate any excess food or clothing which was donated to the needy people, with our consent. I was given any medical treatment which I needed and I do not blame the government for the loss of my............or my.........
I further swear that I have not excluded any further important information and that any WAR statements which I have made through television and radio were made by my own choice.
PRINT NAME...
(FIRST) (MIDDLE) (LAST)
SIGNATURE..
DATE............... ....
(DAY) (MONTH) (YEAR)
Failure to sign this statement will result in execution, or torture causing bodily or mental damage.
BY THE ORDER OF THE GUAMINIAN GOVERNMENT
Due to an unregrettable accident causing the death of the above this statement was signed by..................

As the B-25G entered combat it was thought that it would be able to take battle damage better than the D but Geoff P. Engels, a 1962 USAF Academy graduate who went through an air training command class in which 85% of the pilots went to SAC, recalled how things turned out:

'It was originally thought that if the D got hit or punctured its hot air running the systems would hit the wire bundles, hydraulic pipes or anything else and melt them, turning the airplane into an instant ball of soot. As it was, the opposite proved true – when hit at high altitude the 600degC temperatures were down to 240degC and the high pressure then escaped and expanded, resulting in rapid cooling.

'Also on the D as long as one engine was running, the systems would work but in the G when an engine was lost, everything attached to it went out as well. The G had no hot air ducted from the engines to run its systems – it was all hydraulically and electrically hooked to the engines. It was all the opposite of what the wizards figured when they sent the Gs into battle due to their supposed damage tolerance.'

Above left: The B-52D was modified for service over Vietnam; flying from Guam and U-Tapao, Thailand the Stratofortresses regularly carried 30 tons of iron bombs. *USAF*

Left: This G model is fitted with outboard pylons designed to carry anti-radar chaff propelled ahead of the aircraft by 2.75in rockets, or other diversionary countermeasures systems – which were used often over Vietnam. *Boeing*

Due to the G's efficiency in hauling 27 bombs with full fuel and being able to get back to Guam with more fuel than the Ds (and the latter had refuelled at that while the Gs had not), the Gs were never used out of U-Tapao. All up combat weights for the two aircraft were 450,000lb for the D and 488,000lb for the G.

Geoff Engels went on to recall his first combat tour in B-52s in 1972 – he had already flown combat as a FAC in OV-10s and O-2s, then in EB-66s plus the F-100 before flying 103 missions in the BUFF, bringing his total combat time to 1,482 hours. 'We took our B-52s from Castle to Guam on a 12-hour flight with refuelling' – during this flight the refuelling director lights on the bottom of the KC-135 were hooked up in reverse, leading to some incredible jockying but he got his gas.

Arriving at Guam, Engels went through three over the shoulder SCAT combat training missions, the third being his first solo. As things turned out, that third mission would be unforgettable.

'As the gear was in the wells, the radar went out in the middle of the night in a thunderstorm. We had to fly a "Bonus Deal" mission off the gunner's radar in the aircraft ahead. As we climbed out we had to dodge thunderstorms by the gunner's radar while in a holding pattern.

'We had been briefed that if the bomb run was made west to east, the break from the target would be made to the right after bombs away . . . if east to west, the break would be left. Well, our target got changed on us and we had to make a run over the DMZ opposite to the original target run. We got on the IP and everything was OK – I stayed with my cell and was on the run. The bombs fell off and I forgot which way to turn! I let out a plea over the intercom, "Oh my God, which way do we turn?" There was silence from the crew, then one guy says, "Right, right!" Since that was the original briefed run, I said, "Yeah, right" to myself and turned right.

'The EWO called, "Uplink!", then a visual was called on a SAM – we were turning right into it since I had now penetrated North Vietnamese airspace and was heading deeper north.

'Having been an old fighter pilot and never having believed what I was taught about SAC tactics and how to dodge SAMs, I put that hummer up into about an 85deg to 90deg bank, let it pitch up because the spoilers did that in full tilt and pitch down again and just pulled all the Gs I could on that airplane. And we outmanoeuvred the SAM; watched it go up out of sight – it finally detonated on the ground.

'Then we had to find the flight again. We turned so tight we turned inside of them – boy, did I ever catch a bunch of hell for that one. All those missions were taped and they thought I was the dumbest thing since

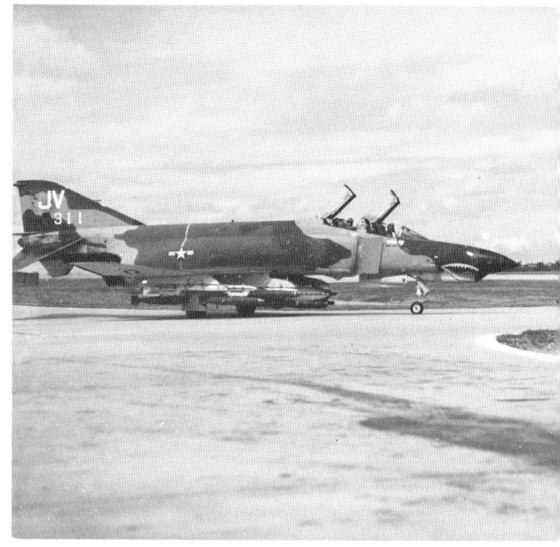

F-4 Phantoms were used in the bombing role in North Vietnam, before B-52s. Three views showing: (*above*) a 388th TFW F-4 taxying out for a strike; (*below*) a pair of F-4s preparing to refuel; and (*right*) F-4Es of 469th TFS/388th TFW bombing over North Vietnam, March 1972. USAF(2); D. Logan via R. Wright

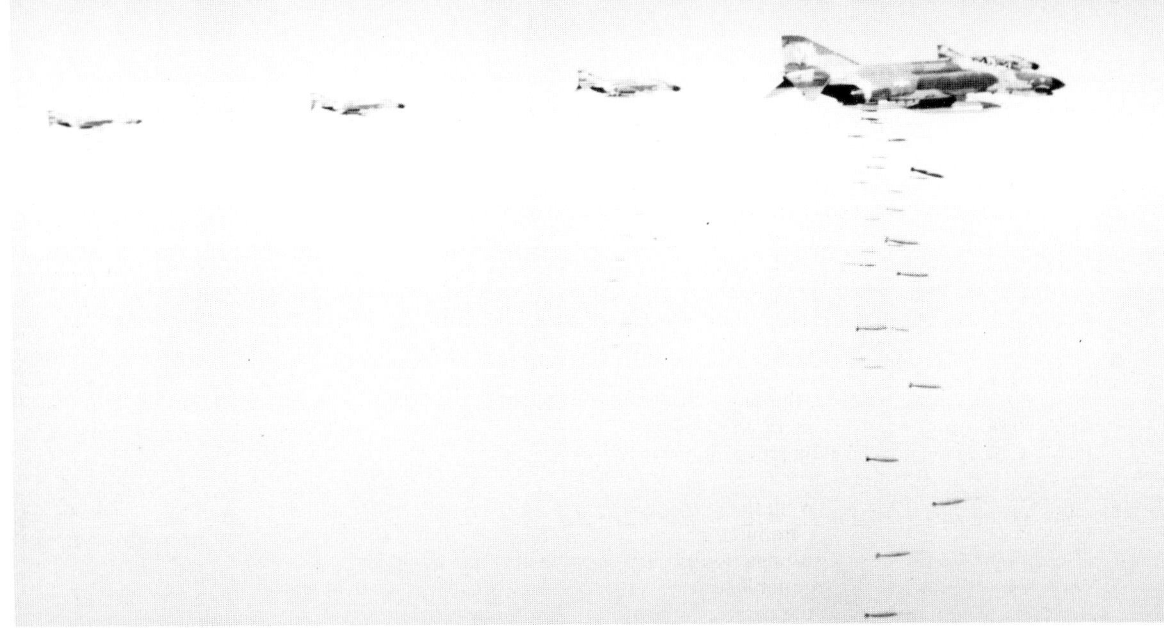

the word go. However, I learned how to dodge SAMs, which served me in good stead later on.'

Geoff's first four missions had three 'Bonus Deals' and his crew always thought of themselves as the 'Bad Luck Crew'. Once on take-off from Guam they had an experience with the infamous cliff, which almost always caused a slight pitch-up as the BUFF passed over it. This time as the gear was coming in there was a tremendous upblast – the nose went pitching far beyond normal limits, so much so that the gunner, Digger O'Dell, was looking at the water. The yoke fell forward at 140kts – they should have been at 162, and Geoff used all 500ft down to the water to recover.

They also experienced night refuelling when the 135 lost its auto-pilot and once needed 88,000lb of fuel in the middle of a typhoon! Ah, the sedate life of the bomber crew.

The tail gunners in the BUFFs had quite an interesting job since they were the only enlisted men on a B-52 crew – the only members that performed the mission of direct defence with a weapon. Howard W. Hoff, still a gunner on B-52Gs with the 68th Bomb Wing at Seymour Johnson AFB, North Carolina, has put over 9,000 hours in the air as a SAC gunner since 1950. Starting on B-29s in Korea, he went on to B-50s, B-36s (with 35-hour missions that were actually comfortable), then B-52s in 1958. Going to the B-52 from the 36 was a real step down in crew comfort but he found the B-52D ideal at high altitude with an isolated crew station. The D at low altitude, however, is an entirely different story – Hoff has gone to the hospital once due to being severely buffeted at low level and has gone through many cracked helmets.

For 'Arc Light' he preferred the D due to the gunner's ability to call SAMs visually to help the pilot manoeuvre. In the G and H models, though, crew coordination was easier since the gunner sits next to the EWO, his electronic counterpart.

Hoff recalls the first time he saw SAMs fired at his BUFF over the DMZ . . . one went off level with his station in the tail and it looked like a garbage disposal was being thrown at him. If the cell coming back ahead reported no missiles, then a knot would start in his stomach since the next cell almost always got shot at.

Tactically Hoff thinks the B-52s suffered in trying to avoid the SAMs – it almost always ended up every man for himself as the bombers continued to fly the same routes in and out of the targets. The radars on the B-52s were going down a great deal and he remembers leading a double 'Bonus Deal' for two BUFFs behind whose radars had quit.

As to the take-offs from Guam, Hoff hated them: 'We used the overrun on both ends and when we hit the gravel on the other end, it sounded like BBs being fired at the skin of the aircraft. Then off the cliff we'd go, watching it rise above the tail at times. Once we went off into a thunderhead and the pilot got vertigo.

'The most scared I've been was as a number 3 out of U-Tapao – we turned short to catch the rest of the formation and got caught in weather, emerging as number 1 – the vertical stabiliser of the real number 1 went between the engine pods of our B-52. We must have missed him by feel!

Left: Andersen AFB, Guam at the height of B-52 activity in 1972. There were 30 less parking spaces than there were aircraft, which meant that a force of BUFFs was airborne at all times, launching and recovering continuously. *Henry L. Conn*

Right: As the 1970s came, B-52s were in the middle of it over North Vietnam. In preparation for Operation 'Bullet Shot', this B-52G at Beale AFB, California taxies out to deploy to South-East Asia on 15 April 1972. *USAF*

'The 100mm AA would not reach the B-52s as a rule but every now and then they would find a peak of 6,000ft or more and catch the BUFFs by surprise.'

'Linebacker' was continually escalated as Nixon attempted to stem the tide of North Vietnamese strength into the South. Imposing a northern bombing limit at the 20th parallel, he sent the B-52s and tactical fighters into the more heavily defended areas and after the monsoon set in, the BUFFs had to make up for the loss of fighter sorties. On 22 November 1972 the biggest mission since April was launched against the southern panhandle of North Vietnam.

Over Vinh a B-52D flown by Capt Norbert J. Ostrozny, on TDY from Dyess AFB to the 307th Strategic Wing at U-Tapao, took a SAM hit that badly disabled the bomber. Even though the return trip was 400 miles, the crew had no desire to get out over the North and they decided to try and make it back, at least to the Thai border. Struggling south, the bomber continued to lose altitude and just over 100 miles away from the target, Ostrozny gave the order to eject at 15,000ft.

In the darkness below 1st-Lt Michael E. Humphreys was on his second flight as a CH-53 Aircraft Commander out of Nakhon Phanom, a night reconnaissance. Humphreys' job was that of dropping CIA trained indigenous personnel into Laos during the small hours of the morning or late evening. Just after take-off, over the perimeter of the base, the tower radioed and asked if his 'Jolly' was the cause of the disturbance on Guard (emergency) channel. Switching from Main to Guard, Humphreys heard the eerie sound of several emergency beepers which are normally activated by ejection.

Heading south, the crew of the 53 saw what looked like starshells going off – they found out later these were the ejection seats of the B-52. The rotating beacon of a fast moving aircraft passed under the helicopter, itself at about 2,000ft above ground level – another mystery that was later found out to be the F-105 'Iron Hand' Weasel acting as escort for the crippled bomber. At the time, however, Humphreys assumed it was something like an F-4 and that this was the aircraft in trouble.

Placing the Jolly in a hover, Mike had the crew get the spotlights on as well as the landing lights and by sheer chance they saw a man land with his parachute – he could have come right through their rotor blades since he was directly in front of them. Over Guard 'Over here, Jolly, over here!' was transmitted and Mike was able to navigate to the downed crew by their individual survival strobes. Hovering by focusing the spotlight on an object on the ground to avoid vertigo, Mike came down among the trees and proceeded to pick up Adam Rech, the Radar Navigator. When Rech was aboard he told the crew it was a B-52!

In a hover most of the time, Humphreys and his crew picked up the Navigator, Bob Estes; the EWO, Larry Stephens; and the Gunner, Ron Sellers. Ostrozny and co-pilot Phil Foley were picked up by a Kaman 'Pedro'. After the rescue was completed, the rescue Jollies arrived on the scene as rescue commanders but there was nothing left to command.

During the rescue the crews watched the B-52 impact the ground, then bounce back up into the air in a tremendous fireball which burned for the rest of the night.

Estes, who had been wounded by the SAM, told of coasting back in with continual flame-outs and restarts until the crew finally got out at 10,000ft. Foley ended up with a broken leg. Ostrozny received the Silver Star from Melvin Laird. Technically the rescue

was not a combat save so Humphreys and his crew did not get decorated – needless to say that was a frustration.

Interest in the mission was strong – this was the first B-52 lost due to enemy action, the ninth in South-East Asia to all causes, in 100,000 sorties. It is interesting to note that the official press release on the shoot-down said the loss of the bomber would not affect American operations or tactics. In less than a month the B-52s and their crews would pay heavily for this as they entered the most demanding phase of their time in combat.

By October 1972 peace negotiations had resumed in Paris but it was obvious the North Vietnamese were playing the cards to their advantage, breaking off the talks on 13 December. Henry Kissinger, in explaining Richard Nixon's decision to hit targets in Hanoi and Haiphong after failure of the talks, said:
'It was decided to try to bring home, really to both Vietnamese parties, that the continuation of the war had its price . . . Once the decision was made to resume bombing, we faced the fact that it was in the rainy season that really the only plane that could act consistently was the B-52, which is an all-weather plane.'

On Friday 15 December 1972 Adm Noel Gayler, Commander-in-Chief, Pacific, warned his commanders to be prepared for the resumption of air operations north of the 20degN in North Vietnam in response to the President's initial directive. Shortly thereafter Adm Thomas Moorer, Chairman of the Joint Chiefs of Staff, notified Gayler and Gen John C. Meyer, Commander-in-Chief, SAC 'that air and naval gunfire operations against targets north of 20degN in North Vietnam would be resumed at approximately 1200Z (1900 Hanoi time) on Sunday, 17 December.' Both commanders were authorised to prepare for a three-day maximum effort by B-52s and TACAIR against essential military and war supporting targets in the Hanoi-Haiphong area – airfield and active SAM sites were included in this to 'improve the effectiveness of the attack forces and to minimise losses.'

Due to the poor weather of the monsoon season, it was obvious the B-52s would play the key role – and this would be the first time the BUFFs would hit targets in northern North Vietnam in strength over an extended period. Typical of the war that was being fought, this would be only the second time in seven years of Stratofort ops in South-East Asia that the aircraft would be employed in a purely strategic bombing role. The first time was the previous April in the five strikes of 'Freedom Train'.

This resumption of 'Linebacker' operations was also to include the fighters, such as Navy A-6 Intruders operating off three 7th Fleet carriers in the Gulf of Tonkin and Air Force F-111s out of Thailand, providing round the clock night and all-weather strikes.

For the renewed bombing up North, the JCS authorised 14 targets for the three days of B-52 strikes by the 8th Air Force. SAC responded by outlining 321 sorties, the majority (129) to be flown on Day 1, 17 December. The plan was not total destruction of any single target or group of targets, but a requisite level of damage effectiveness to meet the objective. Tactics were to be based upon the normal 'Arc Light' cell of three aircraft but with the cells compressed to put more aircraft over the target area more quickly. Almost all the fragged routes into the targets were planned from the west and north-west to take advantage of the high prevailing tail winds. Each wave was to attack four hours apart to provide the

psychological impact of continuous bombing but this, planners acknowledged, would also give the enemy time to recuperate and reload their missile launchers.

Less than two days before the operation was to get underway, the JCS moved the operation back one full day to 18 December at 1200Z as the first TOT (time over target) and on 16 December the JCS notified the participating commands that the nickname for the operation would be 'Linebacker II'. With some changes in planning, the 129 B-52s would be grouped in three waves the first day – 42 D models from U-Tapao, 33 D models and 54 G models from Andersen – with the first wave of 48 Stratoforts over target at 1245Z (1945 Hanoi time).

Early on the 18th, Adm Moorer informed Adm Gayler that, 'You will be watched on a real-time basis at the highest levels here in Washington. We are counting on all hands to put forth a maximum, repeat maximum, effort in the conduct of this crucial operation.' The phrases certainly had their roots in an 8th Air Force of 1943-44.

Bob Jacober recalls that this was just the feeling generated in the preparations and initial briefings for 'Linebacker II': 'it was right out of TWELVE O'CLOCK HIGH.' There was a stand down period before the missions were briefed and all off-base privileges were revoked, particularly drinking, until further notice from the evening of 17 December on. There was a great deal of tension in the air with several unusual rumours (or lack of them). The usual '15th of the month' rumour that G models would be leaving in mid-month did not make the rounds in December and the wild guesses were flying – nuclear missions, orbit or strike China, pave North Vietnam, everyone was going home since the peace treaty would be signed soon and on it went.

Secrecy was stricter than at any previous time in the war – the crews were called to top secret briefings that

Above: June 1973: with the war in South-East Asia just ending, the BUFF was getting a facelift by the addition of the Electro Optical Viewing System. The system enables the pilots to see the terrain via a TV camera or an infra-red sensor. This 410th Bomb Wing B-52H was based at K. I. Sawyer AFB, Michigan at the time. *USAF*

began with the words, 'This briefing is classified Top Secret. Is the room secure?' When the drapes were drawn back from the strike maps Bob and several others did not comprehend the HAN on one side of the map and the OI on the other until the briefer said, 'Gentlemen, your target for today is Hanoi.' The reaction in some rooms was utter silence and in others cheering – the gravity of what was going to happen was evident either way and many felt that at last something effective to possibly end the war was afoot.

The fighter pilots who would be escorting the B-52s in and who would also be hitting targets in Hanoi were elated but they had grave reservations about the Stratoforts going in with inflexible tactics. One pilot of the 13th Tactical Fighter Squadron recalled, 'I can remember the comments made when we realised that the BUFFs were going to attack in successive waves, using the same route all night. Fighter pilots are not quiet, and they let their feelings about SAC come out during the briefing, especially the guys who were going to fly close escort with the BUFFs.'

At 1451hrs, 18 December 1972, the first B-52 lifted-off from the runway at Andersen. One hour and 43 minutes later the 87th BUFF had followed. They would soon be joined by the 42 Stratoforts from U-Tapao and fighters from Nam Phong, Udorn, Ubon, Takhli and Korat. The F-111s flew single ship up the Red River Valley preceding the B-52s to hit enemy airfields. The Marine F-4s from Nam Phong were up to form a MIGCAP escort for the tankers from Taklhi and Okinawa. Chaff was being dropped in large quantities and several other Air Force MIGCAP were set up. Four Wild Weasel F-105s set up an orbit next to the planned B-52 route – certainly more were needed.

The first target struck by the B-52s was Hoa Lac Airfield 20 miles west of Hanoi – six Ds from U-Tapao released their bombs beginning at 1243:48Z (1943:48 Hanoi time). The first three in, Snow Cell, had two SAMs launched at it by the four operational sites while Brown Cell was left alone . . . at least by the SAMs. A MiG-21 attempted to intercept Brown Cell and one of its tail gunners, S/Sgt Samuel O. Turner, picked up the challenge as the MiG tracked the force outbound from the Target:

'Our navigator told us the reference point was in our area and before long we learned the enemy fighter had us on its radar. As he closed in on us I also picked him up on my radar when he was a few miles from our aircraft.

'A few seconds later, the fighter locked on to us. As the MiG closed in, I also locked on him. He came in low in a rapid climb. While tracking the first MiG, I picked up a second enemy aircraft at 8 o'clock at a range of about 7½ miles. He appeared stabilised – not attacking us, obviously allowing the other fighter room to manoeuvre and conduct his run first. As the attacking MiG came into firing range, I fired a burst. There was a gigantic explosion to the rear of the aircraft. I looked out the window but was unable to see directly where the MiG would have been. I looked back at my radar scope. Except for the one airplane out at 8 o'clock, there was nothing. And within 15 seconds, even he broke away and we lost contact with him.'

The kill was confirmed.

The very important Kinh No storage area, nine miles north of Hanoi, was scheduled for attacks during each of the three waves of Day 1. It had over 7,900ft of track and served as a loading yard – the North Vietnamese had 11 operational SAM sites in the area as well as light to medium AAA. Six cells dropped their bombs beginning at 1301Z (2001) and ending at 1312Z (2012). All cells encountered heavy SAM activity inbound and outbound. Lilac 03, a B-52D (56-0678), took a SAM hit 20 seconds prior to release and was not able to drop its bombs but it did recover at U-Tapao.

The final target of Wave I, Day 1 was the Yen Vien Rail Yard, hit by three cells from 1314Z (2014) to 1318Z. Eight SAM sites and heavy AAA were throwing up a barrage and a minimum of 17 SAMs were fired – it was like the 4th of July according to the crews, and this was only the beginning.

Between 1245Z (1945) and 1318Z, 45 of the 48 planned B-52 sorties dropped their bombs – all 21 Ds from U-Tapao, eight of nine Ds and 16 of 18 Gs from Andersen. The SAMs downed one B-52G and badly damaged another Stratofort.

Wave II mustered only 12 Ds and 18 Gs from Andersen, hitting Yen Vien, Kinh No and Gia Lam from 1700Z (2400) to 1726Z. One G was severely damaged, crashing in Thailand after the seven crewmembers baled out.

Wave III was targeted on Hanoi Radio, led by 21 B-52Ds from U-Tapao dropping from 2143Z (0443) to 2158:08Z. The Hanoi Railroad Repair Shops/Gia Lam were struck for the second time on Day 1 by 12 Ds and six Gs out of Andersen – the six cells dropped their bombs from 2207Z (0507) to 2215Z and this time the defenders were more than ready. Two MiG-21s tried to intercept the force inbound without success and at least 61 SAMs were fired. Rainbow Cell alone reported 15 visual SAMs in the target area and Rainbow 01 was hit, making it back to U-Tapao with slight damage.

It did not take long for the North Vietnamese to plot the courses of the inbound bombers since all were flying the same headings, speeds and altitudes in

to the targets with the same turn outbound. Well over 200 SA-2 missiles were fired for the loss of three BUFFs – two over Hanoi and the one that crashed in Thailand. The crews that ejected over Hanoi and were captured were made to give speeches; there were some MIAs.

In a message during the early hours of 19 December, Adm Moorer authorised the continuation of 'Linebacker II' beyond three days with at least 30 B-52 sorties a night against targets in North Vietnam and continuing strikes against the lower route packages to keep constant pressure on southward logistics movements. SAC planners also moved the TOTs (times over targets) from two to four minutes between cells, lengthening the duration of the attack. Day 2 was to consist of 93 sorties, again in three waves.

Wave I on 19 December, Day 2, went back to the Kinh No Complex with its four separate targets. Seven cells from Andersen, 12 Ds followed by nine Gs, hit the area between 1309Z (2009) and 1322Z. Wave II, a mixture of 21 Gs from Andersen and 15 Ds from U-Tapao, bombed Bac Giang Transshipment Point and Hanoi Radio with almost simultaneous TOTs beginning 1650Z (2350). Post strike photos of Hanoi Radio revealed two buildings destroyed and 10 others damaged in addition to five barracks and other storage and administration buildings. The target was dropped from the list for the remainder of the campaign. Two BUFFs, a D and a G, were damaged by SAMs on the 19th while over the target.

Wave III hit the Yen Vien Complex and the Thai Nguyen Transshipment Point with 30 Ds and six Gs from 2210Z (0510) to 2222Z. Ninety of the 93 sorties for 19 December were completed.

The initial effects of 'Linebacker II' were far ranging. The North Vietnamese screamed that the Americans had now lost their chances of a negotiated peace due to the escalated attacks. The POWs in the Hanoi Hilton began cheering as soon as they heard the huge bombs hit the ground – they knew just the opposite would be the case if the bombing was continued. Crews were excited about doing the job the way it should have been done from the beginning of the war but they were also becoming alarmed at the lack of any variation in tactics to avoid being shot down. The eyewitness reports of one of the first shootdowns were unnerving – when the SAM exploded under the BUFF, the aircraft burst into flames and entered a flat spin to drift 7½ miles to earth like a flaming leaf. Pilots were also disobeying directives not to manoeuvre against the SAMs – one pilot manoeuvred at his bomb release point on the way in to Gia Lam Railyards. Four seconds past his release point he finally got wings level and released his bombs – they sailed right down on the Gia Lam Airport, a forbidden target, crashing into the terminal and runway. Since the field was 'civilian' it

Above left: Taxying out at V-T, Thailand. The paint looks pretty good on 55-0608. Often the 400lb of camouflage had to be patched and patched before the aircraft could go through the paint shop. *Robert Johnson*

Left and below left: February 1969 – BUFFs just getting out of U-Tapao. *US Army*

Below: Airborne and on the way into the target the B-52 provided quite a large target. With the bomb bays open, the radar signature became even larger but this was not a problem until the missions over and above the DMZ into North Vietnam. *USAF*

was off limits but crews were delighted that the MiGs normally launched out of the field would now have some trouble.

On Day 3, 20 December 1972, all three waves were scheduled to hit the Gia Lam Railyards with a total of seven cells – the first cell of the first wave was over the target at 1300Z (2000). The North Vietnamese were waiting and the first wave was literally blown apart. One B-52 was shot down by SAMs over Yen Vien and several BUFFs were heavily damaged. Losses were so severe that cells one and two of Wave II, 6 Gs from Andersen, were cancelled and diverted away from the Gia Lam sector without dropping their bombs. Another B-52 was shot down out of Wave III. Only 90 of the scheduled 99 sorties were effective in dropping their bombs.

On Thursday, 21 December, CINCPAC and SAC staffs were searching for something to give the BUFFs better protection – the result was a greater emphasis on suppression strikes on SAMs just prior to B-52 TOTs. In the meantime, BUFF crews had begun a struggle to change the tactics employed through letters and reports to senior staffers after debriefing, hoping that someone would listen. Bob Jacober recalls going to briefing for Day 3 and hearing about who had been shot down, if any were captured and so it went.

Getting fired at on a regular basis was new to the crews as well – this was not like bombing South Vietnam. As Jacober came in behind several other cells on the 20th, he heard the beepers of numerous crew members who had baled out of the two '52s that went down and got his first glimpse of the spreading red glare of a SAM being launched. As it got closer the exhaust turned yellow, then white. Seven SAMs were launched at Bob's cell, several roaring right by the aircraft. One MiG came straight for the aircraft but went on by without attacking. Some of the other gunners said a few of the SAMs were so close they could read the characters on the side and smell the exhaust! One gunner reported watching a SAM come right up and hit the rear horizontal stabilator, glance off against the fuselage, rumble down the fuselage itself and then head out over the cell!

One fabled MiG encounter was reported. The 21 pulled up behind one '52 and prepared to fire when he noticed he had slid into formation with another BUFF in the cell . . . it startled the enemy pilot enough to cause him to jerk on the stick and fire his missile in the wrong direction.

Day 4 sent the BUFFs back on 21 December along the same routes and this time four B-52s were shot down and several more damaged. Even though the North Vietnamese were salvoing their SAMs, the Americans had become predictable and the word

going around the crews was that the North Vietnamese had a grease pencil mark on their radar scopes – all they had to do was wait and fire all their missiles in one direction, then try a lock-on at the last second to avoid the Weasel aircraft.

The BUFF crews began to turn their frustration loose and the Officer's Clubs at U-Tapao and Andersen became their targets as the losses mounted. Word began to filter around to the other units as the damage mounted. The beginnings of a crew mutiny were seen in angry men being sarcastic and disruptive during the briefings. By the 22nd, aircraft began to abort for imaginary reasons and the flight surgeons reported crew members taking themselves off flying status for 'health reasons', two of them using the term mutiny in describing the situation.

Finally one pilot went public in refusing to fly – he was branded as an anti-war protestor when he actually had no desire to stop flying. He wanted the tactics changed. He was discharged. None of the complaints centred around the morality of the war or the targets – the crews were some of the finest professionals assembled in the Air Force ready to do the job.

On Day 5, 22 December, two more B-52s were shot down. Overall the losses were running only 2% or 3% of the force but the crews were crying out that even these losses were not necessary and that almost total effectiveness could be brought about. A gutsy colonel

Above left: This B-52D is about to take on 89,000lb of fuel in around 17 minutes. It was quite a feather in one's cap to get all that kerosene without a disconnect – it was plain hard work that took a great deal out of the crews. *Robert Johnson*

Above: A five-ton flat bed truck, loaded to the hilt, backs up to the bomb loading station of a B-52D from the 4258th Strategic Wing at U-Tapao, February 1969. *US Army*

at U-Tapao, where morale was suffering the most due to crews in the force going out every day without a day or two off, stood up and tried to pass on aircrew complaints to higher echelons but he was 'shot down' for his audacity in thinking that anyone had to correct the tactics that were being flown. Certainly it must be appreciated that the SAC planners had their hands full. Mission results and debriefings would push right into the take-off times for the next mission and things were happening fast enough to see a lag in improvement . . . but one must recall that there were seven straight days of 'going up North' without a change in how things were done. Well over 100 SAMs were being fired per mission and most of the BUFFs seemed to take the heaviest losses as they made their turn away from the target.

This turn was always made in the same direction by each successive cell and when the '52 turned, most of the ECM gear became ineffective until level flight. The North Vietnamese seemed to aim their missiles at this point in the sky with devastating results.

Day 6 and 7 were the toughest for the crews to fly. Morale was at a very low point and most felt defeated – but they kept on flying and SAC planners were now busy changing tactics. There was simply no choice if the 'Linebacker II' campaign was to complete its proposed stopping of the North Vietnamese war effort.

On 24 December, Day 7, the six cells pressing in to the Thai Nguyen rail yards had 19 SAMs fired at them. Black and Ruby Cells were engaged by MiGs. At 1256Z (1956) A1C Albert E. Moore in Ruby 03, a B-52D, picked up a fast moving bogey on his scope. After telling the crew to drop chaff and flares, he got a lock-on at 4,000yd. When the bandit got to 2,000yd Moore opened fire – the blip blossomed on his scope and disappeared. The MiG-21 was seen falling in flames. Gunners claimed another three kills but only Moore's and Turner's of the 18th were confirmed.

By the time Day 7 was over, SAC had admitted to the loss of 11 B-52s in combat – there were several more that had made it back but were useless due to extensive damage. The damage in North Vietnam was extensive and almost every aircraft was able to place its bombs on the designated targets without hitting the civilian population per se. Many civilians were killed near the targets but North Vietnam was

claiming the '52s were 'carpet bombing' the Hanoi/Haiphong area. This was far from the truth. The crews from 307th and 43rd Strategic Wings, flying their D models from U-Tapao and Andersen, and the 72nd Wing flying Gs from Andersen, were doing a highly professional, effective job in the face of the heaviest anti-aircraft system ever thrown at a bomber force. The 400 other USAF and Navy fighter-bombers flying strikes daily along with the BUFFs were doing a remarkable job as well.

With Christmas came a 36-hour bombing halt. 8th Air Force regrouped tactically and physically to prepare for the remainder of what would become known as the '11-Day War'. This time seven waves of Stratoforts would converge on Hanoi at the same time from several different directions and the lead cell in each wave would have the same TOT – 1230Z (1930) . . . and the last cell in each wave would have to have the same TOT as well.

On Day 8, 26 December 1972, 117 B-52s made their way to North Vietnam. For 13 straight minutes bombs pounded targets in Hanoi and Haiphong with awesome results. One B-52 was lost after trying to make it back to U-Tapao – it crashed just short of the runway, killing four of the crew, the first confirmed casualties out of the B-52 force since the rest had been lost over the North. Bob Hymel, co-pilot on the aircraft, recalled the harrowing mission, the crew's fourth.

As the B-52 exited the target area north of Hanoi two SAMs came up behind and to the right and exploded, 'it felt like a kick in the pants, and all of a sudden we had fire lights in numbers seven and eight. I throttled back on seven and chopped eight off while the pilot called the navigators for the shortest route to the ocean so we could bale out if necessary.' The gunner reported flames from the burning engines reaching back past his position and that he was wounded.

After reaching the Gulf of Tonkin, the pilot headed south to reach a base big enough to land the BUFF. The aircraft was streaming fuel from hundreds of

Left: By 1972 Operation 'Bullet Shot' brought additional B-52s into the theatre, including the newer B-52G, as operations over the North were laid on again. This scene at Guam shows Ds and Gs starting up and taxying out in one long line. *USAF*

shrapnel holes . . . three times during the next hour and a half, the crew took on fuel from three different tankers while going for U-Tapao and the best hospital available. Both the pilot and the co-pilot had to fight the controls to keep the '52 level. As the stricken bomber was on final for U-T the tower orderd a go-around but a few hundred feet out the aircraft went out of control:

'As we entered the flare, the airplane just seemed to fly itself away from the runway, yawing hard to the left. Maybe some cables popped or something. Anyway, we came in with the power and nose came up in the air . . . the pilot came on the radio and said, "The airplane won't turn to the right!"

'Then it seemed like it came back that way, to the right. We were using the outboard throttles to create some asymmetrical thrust.'

Pulling the throttles off, the pilot tried to set the '52 down where it was to no avail. Then he added power to gain enough altitude for ejection – the navigators, who ejected downward, needed at least 400ft.

'It seemed like the airplane was pointing straight up in the air, with the altimeter winding up and the airspeed indicator going in reverse . . . I decided it was time to jump out of the airplane and I came over the intercom and said, "Bale out! Bale out!" I reached down and pulled my arming levers up and we hit the ground.'

Bob was knocked unconscious. Other B-52 crew saw the bomber pitch up, then hit the ground tail first and explode. One of the pilots watching, Maj Brent Diefenbach, leaped out of a crew bus, climbed through the perimeter cyclone and barbed wire fence, and grabbed a passing Thai minibus to drive to the burning bomber.

Getting to the forward fuselage, he found the co-pilot's hatch blown away, crawled through the flames and pulled Hymel out. The gunner managed to knock the rear gun turret off and hobble away on wounded legs.

At the front gate of the base the U-T fire trucks and crews were being held on base! When angry crew members demanded an explanation at the crew meeting the next day, they were told the staff had decided to keep the fire equipment on base because other crippled bombers might arrive in need of the equipment. Diefenbach was brought to task for his violation of SAC regulations but an official reprimand was withheld due to the mass opposition of the crews. SAC red tape was certainly legendary.

On the whole, the new tactics were very effective. Although at least two BUFFs were downed, SAM suppression had a great deal to do with holding losses down. Navy and Air Force fighters launched strike after strike and several B-52s were fragged to hit the sites as well. This carried over into Day 9, 27 December, as SAC planned to strike 10 targets with six bomber streams – six SAM sites were on the BUFF target list.

SAMs were as prevalent as ever, though, as the BUFFs pressed toward their targets. One crew, that of Capt John D. Mize, dodged around 25 SAMs in three or four minutes, seeing 15 airborne at once. Ten seconds after bombs away, they were hit and every crew member was wounded. They finally had to bale out – Mize got the Air Force Cross, the rest of the crew received DFCs and Purple Hearts.

The last B-52, the 15th acknowledged by SAC, was lost on Day 10, 28 December and on the 29th, Day 11, the last mission of 'Linebacker II' was flown. Another 14 B-52s were so badly damaged or had crashed on landing so as to be useless, bringing total losses to 29. Twenty-six of 29 approved targets in North Vietnam had been hit.

Geoff Engels, happily flying G models at Loring AFB, Maine after his previous SEA tour, was scheduled to be on alert Christmas day When the squadron CO asked if anyone wanted to be off alert for the holiday the Friday morning before Christmas it was not purely a generous gesture. The day after Christmas Engels and his crew left as the patch up or 'Christmas Help' contingent. Jack Atterbury, the gunner, volunteered to go on the trip so he could get 'his' MiG.

As things turned out, Engels and his men ended up Tail End Charlie for the 11-Day War as the last aeroplane in the last cell over the North. Engels' account, taped for the author, stands as a vivid testimony to what it was like from the crew compartment of a BUFF:

'Coming in everything was normal-normal. We could see the AAA, missiles, bombs going off, cells of aircraft. When we finally got there all the Navy jamming support had gone home, the chaff had blown away and the mutual support from the 60 airplanes ahead of us was gone because they were out to sea by now and we were there by ourselves, about

Above: A SAM site in North Vietnam. Once the BUFFs began to go up North, enemy fire began to damage the aircraft. The greatest threat was from the surface-to-air missiles dotting the enemy landscape. *USAF*

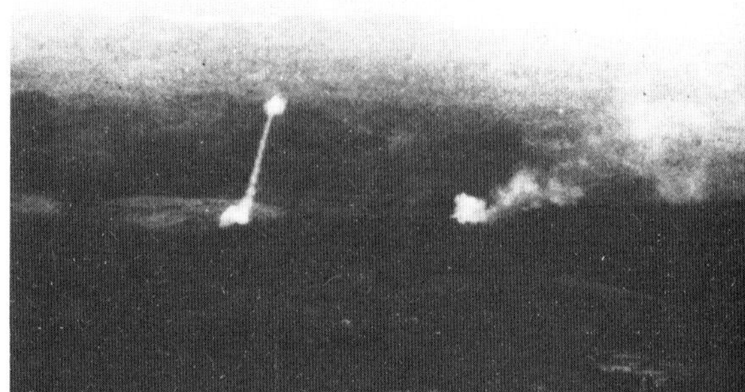

Right: A SAM is launched. Once the radar in the site came on, the EWO aboard the B-52 would call it out. Launch was also called out and with an aircraft the size of the 52 not much could be done with evasive manoeuvring, although several fighter pilots who flews missions in the BUFF could not resist evading SAMs by hard manoeuvring. *USAF*

Below right: An SA-2 in flight. Once the missile was off the rail, tension was close to unbearable and voices often went up to high pitch in calling out the missiles. During 'Linebacker II' crews often counted up to 30 visual sightings before stopping. *USAF*

Far right: The first B-52 to go down as a result of enemy fire was hit by a SAM on 22 November 1972. Since April the SAM activity had been heavy and the crews were only waiting for one to finally go down. Norbert Ostrozny and his crew successfully ejected over Thailand and most of his crew was rescued by Mike Humphreys' CH-53 crew out of Nakhon Phanom. Here the Head Flight Surgeon at NKP, Lt-Col Lockridge, and another flight surgeon assist navigator Bob Estes from Humphreys' helicopter. Estes was wounded by the SAM burst. *Mike Humphreys*

40 seconds from bomb release – I looked out my left window and damned if there weren't three SAMs tracking me from the left side. Then my co-pilot called out three SAMs on the right side.

'So I just did the only thing I knew to do from flying fighters – I put that hummer, a D model, up on its wing again and did the same old manoeuvre and racked it over as hard as I could. And pulled and prayed. I watched the first SAM explode on my left, the second on the left. But that third was not moving on that cockpit – just fire at night – which meant it was coming on a collision course.

'I pulled just about everything I could and let it shudder a little bit and finally that SAM started to move . . . in a hurry. "Boy am I glad that thing is movin'." It vanished underneath the airplane and BLOOEY! I had never heard a SAM explode before and I said, "Damn, that one must have been close!" Radar said, "We're hit!"

'We'd been hit by the third SAM from the left and the third SAM from the right, virtually simultaneously but the damn airplane was still flying so I racked it back up again and believe it or not got back on course and dropped the bombs on target – I don't guarantee our speed was right but we were in the right place on the right heading when the bombs went loose.

'We started back into our SAM evasive manoeuvre, which was ridiculous – a 15° turn with 25° of bank either way. About that time, as we were trying to breathe easy, the gunner screamed he's got three more SAMs coming up at us from the back!

'Torch, our EW, was always so quiet we worried we'd never hear him if SAMs were coming – believe me we heard him when he caught all those signals coming up at us.

' "Three SAMs at 5 o'clock," yelled gunner. Well, nothing else to do but do the same thing all over again, knowing that we have some hits – exact same manoeuvre again, racking it over and pull like a son of a gun and hope the airplane stayed together. It did but the third missile was another close one and it may have put a few holes in us . . . when we got back we had 117 holes in the airplane, all over – the engines, bomb bay, through the belly, some of the seats, HF radio, autopilot.

'The rest of the airplanes were far ahead of us and we went out to sea. The gunner of the airplane ahead of us saw all this and just kissed us good-bye. Guess he didn't know I was a fighter pilot. We called in trying to find out where the rest of the formation was – he was amazed to hear our voices.

'The middle airplane in the cell ahead of us got hit too and he went into Da Nang after taking a bunch of hits. We had fuel leaking out of one of the drop tanks but the engines were still running and everything looked pretty good so we decided we'd head on back to U-T, straight back away from the formation.

'On the way back we kept getting these dumb calls from the ground . . . "Why can't you use the fuel?" . . . "Because the fuel tank has a hole in it." Near U-T the DO came on the line and said he's going to scramble a tanker for us. I said no, that I thought we'd make it. It was too late so we said to let the 135 fly along side and if we needed him we'd tap him.

'We did a controllability check which involved putting the gear and flaps down, putting the spoilers out, making sure everything flies right and handles right down to landing speed. Everything came down and worked fine, strangely enough since we were peppered – my autopilot was knocked out and we had some leaky tanks.

'So we said we were coming on in. The DO countered that he wanted me to take so many thousand pounds in this tank and that tank. I decided I didn't really want to put fuel in tanks or pipes that might have holes. Besides, it was a bad idea to pull gear and flaps back up once they were down so I told him to stand by and I changed channels on the radio and landed.

'After I landed I discovered that SAC colonels didn't like that too well, having captains do their own thinking despite what they said and do what had to be done. Believe it or not he tried to give me a letter of

admonition. I said I didn't think I'd accept his letter whereupon he went in to see the general. The general allowed that they probably couldn't give me a letter and a medal at the same time – they threw the letter in the trash and instead of giving me the Silver Star like the guy at Da Nang got, I only got a DFC. I was being punished. SAC takes care of its own.

'Our gunner, Jack Atterbury, had ridden through this horror show over North Vietnam and that he completely forgot about getting his MiG. He said I made him seasick when I flew . . . I don't understand that. To the best of my knowledge, those last nine SAMs were the last the North Vietnamese ever fired at anybody. My crew became known as the last of the missile magnets.'

The fact that SAMs were still a problem, though not near what it was the first seven days of the campaign, reflects planners not going after the SAM sites with concerted effort until Day 8 through 10.

During the 11-Day War the B-52s flew over 700 sorties, accounting for over 15,000 tons of the 20,370 tons of bombs dropped. Of the 92 crew members aboard the 15 B-52s that were shot down, 26 were rescued, 33 baled out over North Vietnam and were captured, 29 were listed as MIA and four were killed in the crash at U-Tapao.

The damage inflicted virtually stopped the flow of enemy material South. 80% of North Vietnam's electrical power production and 25% of its petroleum resources were destroyed. There had been nothing like it since World War 2 and its effects were immediate. On 30 December Hanoi agreed to return to the peace tables and by 27 January 1973 a substantive agreement was reached.

The BUFFs continued to hit North Vietnam below the 20th parallel until 15 January with the final B-52 mission flown over South Vietnam on 27 January, the day of the peace agreement. The crew of that B-52 from U-Tapao, commanded by Capt Donald A. Becker on his 200th BUFF mission, carried bombs marked in grease pencil by the maintenance and launch crews – 'Good to the last drop'.

B-52 missions to Laos were to stop by 22 February but cease fire violations brought the bombers back on 23 February and on 15, 16 and 17 April. Rebel Cambodians and North Vietnamese/Viet Cong forces continued to advance on Phnom Penh and the BUFFs were fragged to hit logistics targets throughout the country, as well as gun positions and troop emplacements.

With mounting Congressional pressure, President Nixon halted the bombing with the last mission being flown on 15 August 1973, over eight years after the B-52 had entered combat. Capt Vic Putz and his crew, flying a B-52G out of Andersen, said the mission was routine – the bombs were put on target.

Between June 1965 and August 1973 126,615 B-52 sorties were flown – of these 125,479 reached the target area and 124,532 released their bombs. 55% of

Left: 30 October 1972 – a D model prepares to start up for launch out of U-Tapao during the deployment of BUFFs from Guam during Typhoon Olga. *USAF*

the targets were in South Vietnam, 27% in Laos, 12% in Cambodia and 6% in North Vietnam. When the final tally of losses was made, 17 Stratoforts had been lost in combat, all over North Vietnam.

Even with the criticisms that can be levelled at use of the strategic bomber, there remains little doubt that when the B-52 was finally employed as a strategic weapon during the 11-Day War, it brought an end to the war. As early as 1965 military leaders tried to convince President Johnson that a series of swift aerial blows against 94 targets in North Vietnam and the mining or bombing of Haiphong harbour would being an end to the war . . . this was before the vast expansion of ground forces in South Vietnam.

This plan was put before the Senate preparedness investigating sub-committee in mid-1967 and the panel charged that Robert S. McNamara, then Defense Secretary, had continually overruled this military judgement to follow a strategy that was failing. With the hindsight always available to the historian, those vast shifts in defence thinking in the 1960s in the US will continually be analysed. Most of what was done then is being looked upon as detrimental to Western defence philosophy.

Men who had to rise through SAC's lower echelons under a defence department with McNamara's influence saw great intransigence at the upper staff levels. Dana Drenkowski, a USAF Academy graduate, had been used to the willingness to discuss and change tactics when flying with Tactical Air Command to make the mission more effective. When he flew B-52s with SAC in South-East Asia, he attributed what he found in the upper levels to McNamara's company 'yes man' mentality . . .

'During a tour in South-East Asia, I participated in a three-month operation against the highways and passes of the Ho Chi Minh Trail in Laos. For several weeks, flying the same monotonous routes into the same target daily, I (and other crewmembers) reported the introduction of 85mm and 100mm cannons along our route. Since this report would indicate to SAC staff and the Defense Department that the North Vietnamese were equalling our escalation of the war (thus negating the effect of the escalation and, ultimately, discrediting the American administration's policy), this was the type of news that must not be true because it would indicate that our new policy wasn't going to work . . . Intelligence officers would blandly tell us to our faces that what we were telling them did not exist – we must have imagined the airbursts, or we had mistaken lesser calibres of AAA, which couldn't reach our altitudes, for the 85mm and 100mm cannons.

'Our requests to change our course by as little as five miles, which would render the cannon ineffective until the North Vietnamese moved them again, were ignored.'

Six weeks later photographic intelligence bore out the presence of the cannons but changes in the routes 'would have to be made at HQ SAC, at Omaha. Throughout that particular operation, the course, altitudes and airspeeds were never changed. We had to rely entirely on our EWO's ability to jam the AAA radars.'

Two months after 'Linebacker II', Drenkowski visited U-Tapao to interview the crews who flew the historic missions and he was able to gain an audience with one of the senior officers on base. Drenkowski related the stories of the crew mutinies and the problems, asking about some possible ways to improve things. The answer was indicative of the problem . . . 'in the fighter forces, you all have weak staffs, so you and the crews have to ask each other for ideas and help to get the job done. But here in SAC, we have strong staffs. We don't need to listen to the aircrews.'

Needless to say, this was not indicative of the entire staff situation. Many, many officers laid their careers on the line to change things, from lieutenants on up – some were passed over for promotions and they were forced to leave the service. Many senior officers had never heard the stories of crew disaffection and crew recommendations or of the sick call epidemics and the refusals of crews to fly. This has been a hard thing for many in the Air Force to face, particularly in light of the success of 'Linebacker II'. The real credit lies in the professionalism and courage of the crews who got the job done and proved the worth of the bomber when used as it was intended.

When the Collier Trophy for the greatest achievement in aeronautics or astronautics in America was awarded jointly to the 8th Air Force, the Pacific Air Force's 7th Air Force and the Navy's Task Force 77 for their combined efforts in the 11-Day War, most realised the trophy belonged to the men who had flown in the most hostile anti-aircraft environment yet encountered in aerial warfare.

Soldiering On

Ever since the Strategic Air Command (SAC) was created in March 1946 its primary weapon has been the manned bomber. SAC's first commander, Gen George C. Kenney of World War 2 5th Air Force fame, began with a force of 36,800 men and 600 aircraft, including about 250 vintage B-17s and B-29s. By 1948 the B-36 and B-50 were delivered and crusty Gen Curtis E. LeMay took command. Inflight refuelling was also introduced, giving SAC's bombers true intercontinental range.

The Korean War was SAC's first taste of combat as B-29s dropped 167,000 tons of conventional bombs to destroy every strategic target in North Korea within three months. In August 1953 the Soviet Union exploded its first hydrogen bomb and the nuclear arms race started in earnest.

In 1955 the B-52 joined the inventory along with the B-47 and the all-jet KC-135 replaced the KC-97 as the USAF's primary aerial tanker. By the end of the 1950s one third of the bomber force was on 15-minute ground alert and a number of aircraft were on 24-hours a day airborne alert in the US and overseas. By 1968 the airborne alert concept was cancelled due to a number of reasons and today the SAC bomber and tanker force can have as much as 30% of its aircraft on 24-hour ground alert. A peak of 288,000 personnel in 1962 has now dropped to 122,000 (1979) to support just over 1,000 ICBMs and 470 bombers, two thirds of the American strategic Triad made up of SAC's forces and submarine launched ballistic missiles (SLBMs).

In the 1970s SAC went through trying times, as did most of the armed forces in the western nations of the Free World. As budget cuts were made with sweeping regularity, the Soviet Union continued to arm itself since the latter 1960s in the greatest peacetime buildup of nuclear strategic forces in history. This amounted to a 3% per year expansion in real terms or a 45% greater increase than in US forces. 11% to 13% of the USSR GNP was being spent on weapons while the US was spending 5%. This steady investment in the Soviet bloc meant gained momentum with a military manpower force more than double that in the US.

The mainstay of the Soviet arsenal continues to be about 1,400 ICBM launchers backed up by an SLBM force of 60 modern boats with a total of around 900 launchers that regularly patrol the coastal waters of the US. All their missiles are MIRV-equipped (multiple independently-targetable re-entry vehicle) whereas Americans have only the Minuteman III with this capability. Their launch silos are also 'cold', meaning the missile is pushed out of the silo by gasses, then ignited for flight, leaving the silo intact for reloading. Mobile ICBMs have been developed to a great degree as well, requiring only trailers for launch.

The Soviet bomber force of 140 long range bombers and 600 intermediate range bombers – 'Bisons', 'Badgers', 'Blinders' and now 'Backfires' – makes up the remainder of the Russian Triad. The 'Backfire' is the only bomber in production, with another two long range supersonic bomber aircraft in development. About 2½ 'Backfires' are being pushed out of the factory a month. Over 200 have been built so far and there will be several hundred by the 1980s. A new tanker, the Il-76 'Candid' modified transport, is now in service to serve the 'Backfire', making it capable of striking the US and returning to the USSR. Without refuelling, the 'Backfire' could launch and recover in Cuba. The Soviets have continually said that the 'Backfire' is a short range strike aircraft but the 'Fencer A' has fulfilled this role adequately.

Unlike the US, the USSR considers its defensive forces as an integral part of its nuclear forces with 6,000 radars on the periphery of its borders and more inland. While its Tu-126 'Moss' airborne early warning aircraft is not on par with the American E-3A, over 2,600 interceptors back up the warning net while the US fields around 300 interceptors. 12,000 SAMs made up of the advanced SA-5 and new low altitude SA-10 form a formidable anti-aircraft chain and new anti-ballistic missiles (ABMs) are on the way, as well as satellite interceptors in space.

Above right: In 1973, an E model Stratofort, designated NB-5 was fitted with small canards and a nose probe for a series of flight control tests. *Boeing*

Right: Taking on fuel from a KC-135, this B-52H's dark camouflage is a definite disadvantage at altitude. The 'lizard' paint does not become effective until the aircraft is very close to the ground. *USAF*

U.S. AIR FORCE

Closely linked with this defensive force is a major military command in the USSR, civil defence, a command with over 15 generals to protect the population from nuclear attack. $2 billion a year is spent to get 15% of the population and 25% of the work force protected, considering this a nuclear advantage in time of war and an instrument of policy.

A great deal more could be said about the USSR's increasing military capability – general purpose forces, advanced chemical and bacterial warfare, a larger and newer navy and an increase in the quality of their research and development. Opinion is that the USSR and USA are at rough equivalency (1979) but that by 1985 the Soviets will have a clear dominance in military superiority. It is this threat, this environment that the Strategic Air Command, indeed the B-52, must face . . . and survive.

When the B-52 was designed in the 1940s no one had even a remote inkling that its life would be stretched into the year 2000 – a military aircraft with a full half century of service! And yet that is just what is taking place with the remarkable Stratofortress. When the B-1 strategic bomber was cancelled in the 1970s, the manned penetrator role fell back on the 335 B-52s and 65 supersonic FB-111s in the SAC inventory, supported by 600 KC-135s. The arguments have been fielded end upon end as to the viability of the manned bomber in an age of missiles but it has one thing a missile will never have – flexible recall capability. A bomber can be launched in a show of force and then recalled.

As debate continues on a successor to the B-52, if one at all, the venerable BUFF will have to soldier on with continued modification to enable it to perform

Left: Davis Monthan AFB, Arizona, 1971. Over 100 B-52s remain in storage in the dry south-west United States. Most of the aircraft are the old 'tall tails' which could be recommissioned if necessary – in the SALT II treaty, the Russians called for the US to count these aircraft as operational. *Air Force Museum*

Below left: The ill-fated B-1, cancelled in 1978 as a successor to the B-52 due to high cost. The Soviet Union is currently introducing a swing-wing bomber to its inventory with performance similar to the B-1. The US remains in debate over a successor to the Stratofort although a new bomber has been asked for instead of modified B-52. *USAF*

Below: Thinking of the unthinkable. This is SAC's command post located underground at Offutt AFB, Nebraska. From this 'war room' and from others like it in other locations and in the air, SAC will direct its B-52s, FB-111s and missiles in the event the US is attacked. *USAF*

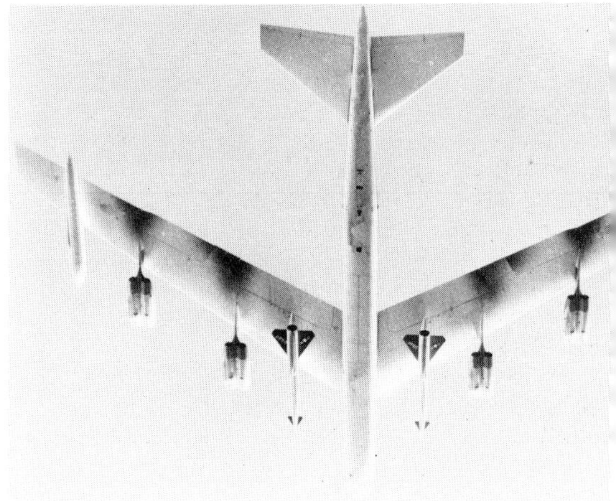

Right: and below: The first cruise missiles, the Hound Dog, are mounted on a B-52G at Edwards AFB, California in May 1960. The GAM-77 became the standard weapon on the Stratofort until the SRAM took its place in the 1970s. *USAF*

Bottom: A B-52G with Hound Dogs – the engines of the externally-mounted missiles could be used for additional thrust if needed, then refuelled in flight before launch. *USAF*

the mission for which it was designed. Considering the last BUFF, a B-52H, was delivered in 1962, the present capability of the aircraft is impressive. Originally designed for an airframe life of 10 years, reskinning and rebuilding programmes have stretched that to five times or 50 years. This is based on 360 flight hours a year for the D models and 370 hours a year on the G and H models . . . or up to the year 2005. Of the 744 B-52s built, 348 were in the inventory as of 1979 with the Ds slated for the conventional role and the Gs and Hs in the nuclear, SRAM and cruise missile role.

The harsh anti-aircraft environment of the nuclear age also forced the B-52 down from its designed high altitude mission right onto the deck for low level penetration, beginning in 1959. With a wingspan of 185ft, low level can be a real experience – watching the wings flex a full 17ft at the tips and the engines travelling in different directions as the pods and wings flex is a genuine jolt. During the early stages of the low level era the aircraft earned the nickname 'Boeing Bounce' from the gunners who had to sit in the tails and get flounced up and down. In 1959 the G and then the H put the gunner up front with a radar set.

As the nuclear environment increased in sophistication the B-52 was placed on an update programme to keep pace – a programme that continues to bring in new developments, particularly in electronic countermeasures (ECM). Part of the BUFFs versatility is its sheer size – there is room for more and more equipment and as miniaturisation increases, so does the room.

One of the first improvements in the aircraft's nuclear strike capability was the Hound Dog supersonic missile, one on each inboard wing pylon. With a range of 500 miles, it gave the Stratofort a stand-off reach and the missile's jet engines could also be fired while unlaunched, adding some thrust if needed. In the late 1970s it was dropped from the active inventory.

As the 1970s drew to a close, the B-52 was the subject of yet more modernisation programmes and additional mission requirements. Word was out that this could only go so far with such an old aeroplane but new life was pumped in the airframe, pushing its life expectancy from the mid-1980s into the next century.

The SAC directives for the B-52 lay in enhanced low level penetration, cruise missile integration and conventional role update. After the 'Pacer Plank' modifications to the B-52Ds, giving them airframe life into the year 2000, offensive and defensive avionics were upgraded as well but the real effort has gone into the Gs and Hs. The expense of maintaining and operating equipment out of the 1950s, with so many parts out of production, was becoming prohibitive.

The majority of the new developments centred around offensive avionics and underwing missile carriage along with the associated electronics. The result would be a pylon that can carry six air launched cruise missiles and SRAMs interchangeably. Kit proofing of the first aircraft was due in June 1981 but there has been a great deal of discussion about cutting off the funds and putting them into a new manned bomber.

The weight savings in the modifications would amount to 1,800lb in the G and 1,900lb in the H. The Bomb/Nav updates would also reduce the circular error probability (CEP) of the onboard missiles by 30-35%. The reduced work load resulting from automation and integration would also reduce the crew from six to five.

The new offensive avionics systems would be digital with improved sensors connected to digital computers. Programmes can be entered into the computer by cassette tape as well. The new sensors include the Honeywell standard precision navigation system, Doppler radar, radar altimeter and attitude and heading reference system. Reliability modifications are also to be introduced to the existing radars.

If Phase 2 of the planned improvements goes through then a second radar altimeter will be added, new forward looking and synthetic aperture radars, radar processor, automatic flight controls and integrated controls and displays for one-man operation of the bomb/nav system. The aircraft will have a nuclear hardened missile launch capability as well.

Defensive capabilities have been continually improved to meet the threat of AAA, SAMs and fighters. Chaff and flares have been standard equipment for some time as has the onboard jamming equipment, but the Gs and Hs were also fitted with smart-noise equipment to counter the Tu-126 'Moss' early warning aircraft. A power management system, ECM transmitter update and a Doppler radar tail warning system are slated for inclusion as well along with several omni-directional antennas for emitting jamming signals.

The end result, called Phase 7, of the advanced defensive system comes to 19 sensors, 5 processors, 17 jammers, flares, chaff and either .50 calibre or 20mm guns (G and H models respectively). And this is only part of what is planned for the BUFF if a new manned penetrator continues to be put on the shelf. (As of 1980 many of these proposed B-52 modifications were to be cancelled in favour of a new bomber.) Kits are being installed now on Gs and Hs for worldwide communications via satellite.

Understandably a great deal of what will be done with the B-52 in the nuclear role will depend upon SALT (strategic arms limitation treaty) negotiations between the Soviet Union and the United States and what is done with both the manned bomber role and the bomber's ability to carry cruise missiles. The latter could be the key since the cruise missile extends the stand-off capability of the B-52 by around 2,500 miles, or the shoot and penetrate mode, using SRAMs after the cruise missiles are away. The cruise missile is also to take the place of the Quail.

The cruise missile, both air and ground launched, came from the recent advances in missile guidance and minicomputer technology. Along with high accuracy the missile can be flexibly routed from launch to impact. The guidance system combines inertial navigation with a terrain contour matching computer which compares preprogrammed topographical features with surface characteristics

Far left: This B-52H nose view gives a good look at the nose modifications installed on all G and H models. The lower bulges house (on the aircraft's right) forward looking infra-red and low level light TV cameras (left). Screens in the cockpit allow the aircraft to be flown visually without reference to the outside. A great deal of ECM gear makes up the rest of the warts and hairs of the aircraft. *USAF*

Below left: A noticeable feature on any current B-52 is the number of bulges and antennae that stick out into the slipstream. These retrofitted pieces of equipment update the BUFF to cope with current ECM and nuclear environment threats. No question these additions have made the aircraft a bit uglier – but better ugly and alive than pretty and dead. *USAF*

Left: Head on view of a B-52G pulling into the tanker. Note that the refuelling receptacle is open as is the left camera door on the nose. *USAF*

Below: Boeing-built ALCM in the bomb bay of a B-52. *Boeing*

which the missile sees in flight, signalling course corrections as needed.

Only 234in long, it is powered by a 600lb thrust turbofan engine, having evolved from the subsonic cruise armed decoy programme of 1972.The B-52G has initially been slated to carry the ALCM, the Boeing AGM-86B, with up to 20 per aircraft, but there has also been study on aircraft modified to be ALCM carriers, such as the Boeing 747 or DC-10. This could have a great deal to do with the future of the B-52.

Since the B-52Ds were rebuilt – the 'Pacer Plank' modifications – (actually wing panel replacement, new fuselage skin and new electrical wiring in the wings), they have been slated for carrying the proven conventional capability of the aircraft . . . but both the G and H have now entered the increased non-nuclear mission phase in the aircraft's history.

In what SAC calls the Collateral Mission capability of the BUFF, there have been several investigations into using the phenomenal range of the aircraft on other non-nuclear missions. Interdiction of the sea lanes, anti-submarine warfare, mine laying and sea surveillance have received the most attention to the great joy of the US Navy.

Since conventional bombing is still favoured, new maintenance practices have allowed, for the first time, B-52s to be simultaneously refuelled, loaded with weapons and given maintenance. Quick Turn checklists can now get a bomber ready for take-off 4.4 hours after engine shut down from a previous mission . . . and the aircraft can fly over 10,000 miles (in the case of the H) without refuelling.

In 1974 the B-52 was tested for the maritime role in identifying and photographing friendly ships with hand-held 35mm cameras and the vertical K-17 camera that was already a part of the aircraft's equipment. 'Busy Observer' training began on 18 August 1975 on 12 bases in the continental US – crews flew missions against Navy designated targets for Navy purposes. During 'Busy Observer II' in August

Left: Scramble! This is what a cartridge start looks like when all eight engines are started at once. This cuts down time to take-off by such a large margin that the BUFFs can get off in minutes. *USAF*

Below left: A B-52G sits alert, chocks behind the rear trucks, ready for instant start. *USAF*

Below: A B-52G gets airborne, gear tucking up in typical opposite fashion. *USAF*

1976 the BUFFs went out and photographed Soviet vessels for the first time.

The mission is flown with a pair of B-52s, one going in low to photograph the target with the other at 15,000ft for mutual support. The low BUFF comes in to within 1,000ft of the vessel. The photos show some very surprised Soviet crewmen.

On 6 April 1978 B-52s from K.I. Sawyer AFB, Michigan intercepted the Soviet aircraft carrier *Kiev* as it passed north of Scotland and then spent three hours with the Soviet fleet, photographing the ships involved in the Soviet manoeuvres. Flying 15 hours from their base, the B-52s were able to make contact in shifts for three separate looks at the fleet.

The B-52 can also carry the 2,000lb GBU-15 glide bomb, three per aircraft, which is guided to its target by a TV sensor at stand-off range. Tests have proven the weapon to be extremely accurate against shipping.

Aerial minelaying has been a part of the BUFF mission since 1974 with the D model being the sole delivery vehicle for the time being. The mines can be delivered down to almost no visibility and ceiling and one BUFF can drop 43 Mk 40s in one go from 400 to 600ft. Up to 80 mines have been carried, as supplied by the Navy, and results have been impressive.

In September 1978 B-52s were slated to test their minelaying mission during NATO exercises in the North Sea. Flying from Pease AFB, New Hampshire, two B-52Ds were airborne for 19hr 30min and put the mines squarely where they were requested.

New mines are being developed for the BUFF, such as the Captor Mk 60, an encapsulated torpedo that can lay dormant for long periods until receiving a signal. As an enemy submarine comes by, the weapon can be activated to seek and destroy – and the B-52 can carry 18 of them.

The author's impression of SAC's enthusiasm for the continuing usefulness of the B-52 was lasting. The HQ SAC personnel at Offutt AFB, Nebraska were hopeful for a new manned bomber to take the place of the B-52 and the FB-111 but they did not see how any other aircraft could perform such a wide variety of conventional missions . . . and perform them with such accuracy. As so many critics have charged, the Stratofortress is not an aircraft in search of a mission.

Far left: This 416th Bomb Wing shot, taken during 'Busy Observer', 8 February 1979, puts the photographer almost on the deck rails. This result is from the hand-held 35mm camera and is considered the worst of the lot – most are crystal clear. *USAF*

Left: This BUFF is getting a close look during a long range sea surveillance mission. With such long range and extensive loiter times, the B-52 has proven to be very effective for the mission. *USAF*

Below: On 6 April 1978 B-52s from K. I. Sawyer AFB, Michigan intercepted the Soviet aircraft carrier *Kiev* north of Scotland, then stayed with the Soviet fleet for three hours, photographing the ships on manoeuvres. The flight from Michigan took 15 hours. This shot of the *Kiev* was made with the 35mm hand-held camera aboard. *USAF*

Bottom: All in all, the BUFF still retains some clean lines, as exhibited by this B-52H in formation with an EC-135. *USAF*

Flying the BUFF

Even by a generous stretch of the imagination, the B-52 is not a 'pilot's airplane'. It is a mission effective weapons platform handled by a crew of professionals that does not think a great deal about the joys of flight. Stratofort pilot H. William Detmer put it this way . . . the aircraft 'has enough aluminium and steel in it to make 20,000 garbage cans. If all the wire and cable were laid end to end it would stretch 100,000 miles. The combined power of its engines is equal to 12,000 locomotives. And it flies like 12,000 locomotives pulling 20,000 garbage cans on the end of 100,00 miles of wire.'

Pilots coming straight out of Undergraduate Pilot Training, where they flew the T-38 Talon – for all intents and purposes a sensitive, supersonic fighter type aircraft – into the B-52 training programme at Castle AFB, California have always had to relearn in order to fly the BUFF. Richard J. Millikin, a B-52G aircraft commander at Barksdale AFB, Louisiana as this is written, recalled what it was like after only one year in the 'Great Green Pollution Machine':

'I am fascinated with the aircraft. That it flies at all, much less as well as it does, is miraculous. The airplane is only two years younger than I am and at the rate it is going it will be here longer than I will. Its design was so far ahead of its time I can hardly imagine that it was built at all considering the tremendous departure from the norms of aviation design at the time of its conception.

'Flying it has been quite interesting if not fun. It does not fly like a real airplane. In 5,700 hours of flying time I had never flown an aircraft over 12,000lb gross weight. Rumbling down the runway for a mile and a half with half a million pounds of JP-4 and recycled beer cans was quite a departure from my background . . . I did two tours in the T-37 as an instructor pilot at Moody AFB and then was a pilot instructor teaching navigator students at Mather AFB.

'My first flight goes down in history since my co-pilot managed to do something that no one had ever seen before without damaging the aircraft. He was making his first landing when he dragged the number 8 engine on the runway. That's been done a number of times – what made it significant is that he did it without damaging the tip gear or the external tip tank. Boeing said it couldn't be done that way and maintenance was sure the wing spar was totalled.

'Since this was our first ride in the airplane and our first attempts at landing it we both had considerable trouble. The BUFF wallows a lot in the landing configuration. Over-correcting is the biggest problem for someone coming from a more conventional plane. One does not attempt a wing low landing since there is so much wing out there on either side of the cockpit. Directional corrections must be done with rudder only which was quite a change for me since the T-37 must be crossed up and slipped in to land with a crosswind. The co-pilot who had just come from T-38s was used to landing in a crab but was not ready to use the amount of rudder pressure required to swing the nose of the BUFF. It's quite a bit. Using that much in the T-38 would have meant a rudder roll.

'The plane landed in a crab but took off for the edge of the runway. He used steering to straighten it up. This caused the wings which were still flying to rock toward the outside of the turn. As the plane S-turned back to the centre line he straightened the nose out. This caused the wings to rock in the opposite direction. This was further compounded by use of the spoilers which amplified the rocking. I think the wing twisted at the tip, allowing the tip gear to swing up and forward as the wing flexed to allow the engine to drag on the ground. Anyway, the plane was not totalled at all and was flying within a week much to everyone's surprise and, I might add, relief.

'That was to be only the first of several problems we would have but the rest were more or less normal. Of our first five sorties, we had four emergency landings; we had one engine eat itself; we had a tip gear that wouldn't come down; we had jammed flaps; we had one incident of split gear. That was quite an experience for me. On landing roll I went to turn off at the end of the runway but nothing happened. I muttered a few garbled expletives but the IP did not interpret them correctly. I slammed on the brakes and plastered everybody against their seat belts. That got the IP's attention. He took the aircraft and attempted to turn it but to no avail.

'After we climbed out of the plane we found the nose trucks were split . . . that is, each was pointing in the opposite direction. A circuit breaker panel cover had broken off and cut the steering actuator cable. I haven't had anything happen to me since I left Castle. I try to maintain my reputation for bringing them back alive.'

Once the fledgling BUFF pilot graduates from Castle AFB and gets into a wing, he takes his place along with five other crew members and gets down to business. The current threat, as the Soviet Union's

Above: The B-52 pressurisation system provides its crew with altitude equivalents of 7,000-10,000ft at operating levels up to 50,000ft. *Boeing*

capabilities are termed, determines the Designed Operational Capability (DOC) of the wing and then the training requirements are broken down into air refuelling, navigation, low level navigation, bombing and instrument and emergency procedures.

The ultimate test of what a wing can do is the Operational Readiness Inspection, the dreaded ORI. This inspection is on the spot and out of nowhere when a team appears on the field from the USAF's Inspector General office. Experts in every field of the aircraft's and wing's operations are tasked to evaluate the wing in a matter of days. The wing commander is put on the spot and he can be 'fired' or kept on. Even though the ORI is supposed to be without notice, most wings get word in advance through the 'grape vine' so they can get somewhat prepared.

One long mission is flown by each crew every six months under a Wing Evaluation or an ORI but most of the continuation training is broken down into quarterly Readiness and Currency Events. The former have to do with performance critical to mission success or alert while the latter deal with flying the aircraft itself.

Fitted into this quarterly programme are a minimum of nine training sorties per crew that will take care of these Readiness and Currency requirements. Each member of the crew receives training critical to his specialty. With the length of time a crew stays up for a long mission – over eight hours – the flying time amounts to 66 hours per crew per quarter.

SAC has been trying to take out some dead time in which no real training is taking place and the sorties are now more event oriented with shorter missions to local training routes. As of 1980 SAC was trying seven event training sorties of five hours each, four mission profile sorties of 7.2 hours each and one pilot proficiency sortie of 2.2 hours (mostly landing pattern practice).

Wings are also trying the 'Cold Seat' swap using one aircraft with two crews. Either one fuel load is used or a quick refuelling is accomplished as the crews swap places – the aircraft does not have to be thoroughly preflighted each time and in little time the next crew is away on a mission.

Without question, from the point of view of crew duty, the most trying aspect of being in SAC is pulling alert – standing by in the heavily guarded alert facility for seven straight days without being able to leave except for special reasons. Families can come to the facility on each base but the visits are usually held in a picnic shelter just outside the alert building and visits are limted.

Up to 30% of the SAC bomber and tanker force is authorised to be on 24-hour ground alert – this normally translates to 14 bombers and 14 tankers on alert per wing parked at the end of the runway ready for immediate launch.

Once launched to avoid nuclear destruction – currently the US doctrine is not to launch until attacked, although this is changing to some degree – the B-52s fly to predetermined orbit points and await orders by the National Command Authorities. The advantage of the manned bomber in a situation like this seems to outweigh its deficiencies. It is flexible in that it can be recalled if the attack is false – a missile, once launched, is committed. If the attack is definite, then the bomber can be retargeted if necessary while in flight. The B-52 carries most of the nuclear hitting power in the Triad for this reason, among others. An orbiting force of bombers is also an effective show of force.

All this is fine as far as doctrine goes but in recent years the USAF has realised that crews need realistic combat training . . . without going into combat. In the mid-1970s, 'Red Flag', 'Blue Flag' and 'Maple Flag' training exercises were set up to place the airman into a combat environment. In analysing the results of the war in South-East Asia, planners found that until 10 combat missions were experienced, a crew member just was not able to cope with the intense environment.

'Red Flag' was the first series of exercises set up, by Tactical Air Command, in the deserts near Nellis AFB, Nevada. An entire threat area was constructed with SAMs, AAA, enemy fighters, enemy troops and all the trappings. Squadrons were sent into this area when deployed from their home bases to face actual combat conditions with the exception of live ordnance. Everything was monitored by computer and printed out at Nellis – gun cameras were used and the enemy equipment, much of it captured, was made operational even to the point of having the SAMs produce a puff of air to kick up dust during a simulated firing.

If crews were 'shot down', they were often trucked back out into the desert to begin escape and evasion from an enemy force in the area. Often rescue helicopters were sent out to retrieve the crews. Air to air combat became alive again as 'aggressor' squadrons painted like MiGs and using MiG tactics came in against the friendlies. With very few limits, the crews flew real combat tactics from zero feet up to service ceiling of the aircraft.

SAC joined the 'Red Flag' system in July 1976 and BUFF pilots, as well as every pilot in the USAF ideally, found themselves in the midst of almost 3,000 missions during a single 3½-week period. Every B-52 wing participates now in every exercise with at least three sorties. Both high and low level missions are flown in support of Army forces as well as in simulated nuclear missions.

In addition to flying true (below 500ft) low level missions, the 'Red Flag'/'Maple Flag' training allows the crews to drop BDU-8 and 38 nuclear training shapes and Mk 82 conventional bombs either live or inert from high or low level. Every crew in SAC must

Above: SAC readiness was a major portion of the US deterrent in the 1960s, forming the majority of the strength in the Triad. These BUFFs at Ellsworth AFB, South Dakota are in the middle of an ORI (Operational Readiness Inspection) under simulated battle conditions – this inspection was the most dreaded since wing commanders were easily made or broken by it. The same could be said for every participant. *USAF*

Above right: A B-52G with a pair of Hound Dogs – gear is just coming up and its landing gear position indicates take-off into a cross-wind to pilots' right. *Boeing*

fly at least one of these missions a year. The results are both surprising and gratifying. After getting one's feet wet, real combat flying is fine tuned. Rick Millikan recalled taking his 2nd Bomb Wing B-52G to 'Maple Flag' in 1979:

'When I participated in a "Maple Flag" mission in Canada we were allowed to do our own thing. This was my first mission of this sort since coming to SAC and I enjoyed it very much. It proved to me that there was some factor of survivability for the BUFF when it comes time.

'We were able to evade CF-101s and F-15s for most of the route. We even took out seven fighters along the way. My mission covered a simulated target on an island in the middle of a frozen lake. That proved to be our downfall – it is virtually impossible to hide the Great Green Pollution Machine over a frozen white lake. I considered rolling inverted but the crew unanimously vetoed that idea.

'Up until the time I turned and nosed out over the lake we were undetected. We had found the fighters' air-to-air freq and listened as they finally picked us out. While I have flown that low before, I have never flown that fast that low before. It was very fatiguing but quite a thrill. We stayed in the ground effect most of the way which made it a very smooth ride despite the ridges and tree tops whistling past in my peripheral vision. After staying down there two and a half hours, climbing out was quite a relief.

'At that altitude radar navigation is quite a trick but my new Radar Nav did a great job – he has been in a rated supervisory job for a few years but it all came back to him when it counted. We got our targets.

'Occasionally the turbulence at low level can be disabling. I have had my hands and feet literally jerked off the controls at times. Normally we don't go in if the winds are over 40 knots in mountain turbulence – the wings start flopping and the engines gallop in different directions. It is a bit distracting but so far we haven't lost many to that cause, at least that I know of.

'Since the B-52 is prone to structural damage at lighter weights, we are limited to a max weight of 420,000lb and a minimum of 250,000lb to enter low level. This is also true when landing it under emergency conditions. Below certain weights the yaw created by asymmetric thrust is uncontrollable at higher power settings. This means that you get only one crack at a landing under certain conditions. To attempt a go around could cause an uncontrollable roll and structural damage.'

Flying with the US Air Force is always a privilege for an outsider. One of the authors has flown with the 68th Bomb Wing at Seymour Johnson AFB, North Carolina twice, once when it was under the command of Caryl Calhoun and again with Henry Conn in command. Both 8½+ hour missions in the B-52G gave an unforgettable first hand look at how the BUFF is used in SAC and how much plain hard work is involved.

Under the 42nd Air Division, the 68th comprises the 911th Aerial Refueling Squadron with KC-135s and the 51st Bomb Squadron B-52Gs. In 1978 the 68th flew 5,432 hours in 672 sorties – the cost was $316 per hour without pilots and fuel for the Stratoforts

and $165 per hour for the Stratotankers. Most of the 68th's cancellations were due to weather and it ended up the top wing in the 8th Air Force that year.

A third aircraft is assigned to the wing, and to all bomb wings in SAC – the T-38 supersonic trainer. This has proven to be a great morale builder and a definite help in keeping the force proficient. The problem of co-pilots not getting enough pilot in command time has long been a SAC concern. The idea of providing a T-38 'flying club' for the 'co's', which they can use at any time it does not interfere with normal duties, was an immediate success. In 1978 68th co-pilots flew 541 hours every three months visiting other bases and generally flying where they wished. Henry Conn says the result has been increased proficiency in the cockpit of the BUFF.

On 1 November 1978 the 68th Bomb Wing, flying as a part of the 'Busy Brewer' missions to Europe, took off from North Carolina and refuelled to make bombing runs in Germany. The missions lasted almost 20 hours and the results were impressive. The trend throughout the USAF is realistic training – fly as if it were an actual combat situation without the many restrictions of peacetime flying.

My flights with the 68th were realistic enough even though I did not have the 'privilege' of sitting on an aluminium box for that long. Eight and a half hours was enough on each flight.

SAC tries to keep each B-52 crew as an intact unit that flies together, pulls alert together and so on. This not only keeps personnel shuffling down but a coordination and ability develops within a team that knows what to expect from each member. My introduction to flying the Stratofort was a two-day briefing! Yes, two days not two hours. It takes this long for a crew to properly plan a mission.

The pilot is aircraft commander. He coordinates the crew, does most of the flying and refuelling and he paces the mission with the aid of the co-pilot. The 'Co' is the BUFF performance officer, taking the place of the old flight engineer in addition to his other flying duties. Fuel must be managed carefully from tank to tank or the centre of gravity can travel out of limits. Take-off data must be computed exactly for the temperature, weight and condition of the airfield. Water injection is a normal procedure for the B-52G's engines, increasing thrust from 10,000lb per engine by several thusand pounds – it takes a great deal to get 488,000lb of aircraft off a runway on a hot day.

Co-pilots are now moving up to the left seat within 18 months, something unheard of a few years ago.

The navigator plans the actual route of the mission from take-off to landing. Using VFR maps without nav aids, he must make exact control times for the bomb run. The aircraft is directed on track, heading and time from his seat. Celestial navigation is also required although it takes some getting used to since the BUFF wallows through the air in dutch rolls. The nav has to shoot his stars when the aircraft is at a certain point in its wallow.

The radar navigator is actually the bombardier although he backs up the navigator as well. His radar enables him to direct the aircraft to the target with uncanny precision for weapons' release. He can also direct the pilot into an airfield on a self-contained Ground Controlled Approach if the nav aids go out and he also finds the tanker's transponder when out of visual range.

The electronic warfare officer (EWO) is on board to buy time to get away from potential enemy threats . . . to keep the BUFF survivable. The B-52 is crammed with enough jamming equipment, chaff, flares (to decoy heat-seeking missiles) and black boxes to keep it in the air to perform the mission but it is slowly becoming hard to service. As this is written

Far left: This B-52G is carrying air-to-ground SRAMs on its external pylons. A total of 20 can be carried (eight in a rotary launcher inside the bomb bay) and launched at different targets several hundred miles apart. Nuclear tipped, they can be re-targeted in flight before launch. *USAF*

Left and below: A B-52G gets up and away like a herd of turtles but with quite a bit more noise. *USAF*

the Phase II update of the aircraft's defensive avionics system is being retrograded down to research and development rather than for fleet installation. Cruise missile installation was also dropped from 20 per aircraft to 12. If this latter decision sticks, then the B-52 will not be able to stand nuclear alert into the year 2000. It will be too vulnerable.

The only enlisted man aboard is the gunner. Sitting next to the EWO, his defensive counterpart, he operates the tail guns through his radar scope – four .50 calbres in the G and a 20mm Gatling cannon in the H. The Ds still have the gunner in the tail but all these models have been configured for conventional warfare alone.

The B-52 is an impressively large airplane for so little crew space. Once inside, the dimensions cramp down so that one cannot walk upright, confining one to a crew seat for most of the time. SAC inflight box lunches and coffee are quite good, however, so the aircraft is not without its comforts. The only passenger seat is the IP seat behind and between the pilot and co-pilot – it does not take long to find out that most of the room in the seat is for the parachute. It moves on rails to the side to allow the crew to leave their seats and go aft.

Both crews the author flew with were more than accommodating in allowing a glimpse of what it takes to make the BUFF perform. The aircraft commanders of both flights, Lt-Col Hugh Wellford and Maj Hugh W. Nixon, Jr, had crews that served in evaluation capacities within the wing.

With everyone in, the behemoth came to life and we taxied out effortlessly due to the landing gear trucks' capability to turn sideways or crab, allowing the B-52 to crab into the wind on landing. Running up the engines, the two pilots looked as if they were playing some multistopped organ.

Take-off and climb out are unique in the Stratofort. As the machine gathers speed the wings flex up, flying before anything else. Then the thing literally hoists its tail and elevates upward with its nose pointed 4° down. The odd attitude is created by the wing incidence. Watching from the ground, one sees this monster rise in blatantly nonaeronautical fashion.

Our B-52G, serial number 58-0170, had 8,058.2 hours on the airframe, certainly a healthy service life. As we rose into the air at 0805hr at a gross weight of 439,000lb, radar vectors were given to Greensboro, North Carolina and flight level 310 (31,000ft) for a

Far left: The B-52 carries a great deal of fuel, even when landing after a lengthy mission. The aircraft is always under a great deal of stress as well in all flight operations, making pilot management of the utmost importance. This Stratofort had to make a crash landing at Loring AFB, Maine and the results speak for themselves. *USAF*

Above left: A Stratofort touches down at Eglin AFB, Florida and is braked with the aid of a drag chute, 8 May 1956. *USAF*

Left: A look at the tremendous spoilers on top of the B-52G's wing and the Fowler flaps. With the G, the aileron disappeared in favour of these spoilers – from the pilot's point of view, the aircraft shudders into a turn and has some turning characteristics that must be anticipated. *J. Ethell*

Below: Terrain-hugging B-52G typifies the mission profile of today's Stratofortress fleet. Originally designed as a high-altitude global bomber, the B-52 has adapted to ever more hostile measures against it. *Boeing*

rendezvous with the KC-135 tanker. The early refuelling has to do with aircraft handling characteristics as the gross weight changes – the lighter the aircraft, the less stability. The controls are peculiar enough and in thin air they require greater input.

'Liner 25, this is Top Hat, do you have us in sight yet?' The tanker was calling and our radar nav had us locked onto the large 135 by radar. Once the tanker was in sight, flying a racetrack pattern, we pulled up and stabilised just below and behind awaiting the signal from the tanker to hook up. Once the BUFF was cleared in the view was incredible – the 135 filled up the windscreen and the direction lights became the central focus of the pilot.

The BUFF moved in ever so gently and the boom operator in the 'tank' plugged the refuelling probe into the top of the fuselage just behind our heads with a very noticeable THUNK. The boom had to be flown down into the B-52 with controls very similar to that of a normal aircraft. Then the work started.

The BUFF must be kept within the limits the boom will flex. There is more leeway than meets the eye for both vertical and horizontal movement but the Stratofort can start moving and get in trouble fast. Embarrassed crews have come home with booms broken off in the fuselage.

In addition to the lights, the boom operator gives a running commentary on where the bomber is going. The final aid to the pilot is a power boost assist on the controls working through the autopilot, greatly easing control pressures.

The work required to stay in position for 20 minutes at a time is more than demanding. The pilot and co-pilot normally take turns plugging in, staying hooked up for 10 minutes at a time, then backing out. The B-52 is a handful as it is but during refuelling it is a monster with a mind of its own. The aircraft demands very large control inputs to move it at high altitude, then equally large inputs to stop it. As I watched this labouring process, both men began to sweat heavily as they peered single-mindedly out the top of the cockpit, moving the controls almost instinctively.

The 135 pilots can feel the bomber approach and plug in even though the tanker is on autopilot. The entire tanker goes 'up' as the air pressure from the BUFF bumps into the rear of the tank – quite a helpless feeling.

The high level bomb runs are made under the radar bomb scoring (RBS) system – a lock on from the ground is made on the approaching bomber, tracking it automatically on a plotting board. Just before the simulated release of the bomb, the aircraft transmits a tone to the RBS site by radio. The point of simulated bomb release is indicated by stopping the tone.

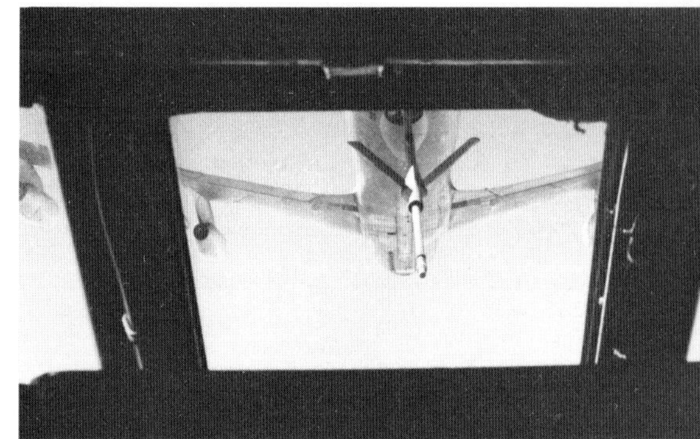

Accuracy is then computed with all the variables figured in.

The real challenge, however, centres around the low level bomb runs since this is how it will have to be done in combat. By 1208hrs we had dropped into the Richmond, Kentucky Low Level Route set aside for military training. With a maximum altitude of 500ft for the runs, made through the Appalachian Mountains, the peaks of the hills were above eye level. With 185ft of wingspan to worry about, the tension is evident but the BUFF does remarkably well in this role, as Rick Millikan recalled.

Left top to bottom: Pulling in to the 'tank' and hooking up to get some juice. The normal procedure is to pull up directly behind the KC-135 and stabilise, awaiting the boom operator's call to proceed. Once hooked up, a BUFF pilot follows the directions of the 'Boomer' and the lights on the forward portion of the 135's fuselage. One set gives fore and aft movement, the other lateral movement. If the lights remain centred, theoretically everything is fine unless, as one BUFF pilot related, the lights are hooked up backward. These shots were taken from the 68thBomb Wing B-52G in which the author flew. *J. Ethell*

Below: This is what it looks like from the other end, out of the boom operator's position aboard the KC-135. Note the deployed spoilers on the right wing. One can literally feel the air deflected by the BUFF bump into and push up the 135. This 68th Bomb Wing crew is hanging right in there. *J. Ethell*

The bomb runs are realistic, complete with simulated AAA, SAMs, fighters and bomb release. The conversation over the intercom on the first run was rapid – 'SAM 12 o'clock – go as low as possible!'

'Stand by for IP, 1min 58sec.' 'Two degrees right.' '1min 52sec to release.' The bomb doors opened at 350kts true airspeed 10 seconds before the first simulated SRAM release, then the tone came on at 20 seconds . . . '5, 4, 3, 2, 1, release!'

'Enemy aircraft at 6 o'clock and 12,000 yards!'

Within minutes we had released three simulated SRAMs to be scored by the RBS, then a fourth as we sailed through Tennessee from Kentucky, down through the mountains for radar evasion.

The second bomb run was made without much time lag after the first. Sitting with the navigators buried in the bottom of the BUFF was a study in precision. The nav controls course by requesting true airspeed and exact time hacks over the ground. Using the radar scope he gets a distinct picture of the ground as it goes by and is then able to make a visual run on the target. The inertial navigation system that is a part of the SRAM equipment can be used by the nav to make his way to the target as well, in addition to directing the missiles. The last two runs on the mission were to drop three gravity weapons and one SRAM.

The pilots were able to make their runs with the TV screens of the EVS when we ran into low fog in spots along the route, allowing us to complete the run as if we had sight of the ground.

By 1445hrs we were flying the BUFF out over the Atlantic, down on the water, in an attempt to

Above: A 68th Bomb Wing B-52G at rest at Seymour Johnson with all the engine bays open for inspection and repair. *J. Ethell*

Left: Jeff Ethell, with the aircraft he flew. 58-0170, a B-52G, belongs to the 8th Air Force's 68th Bomb Wing at Seymour Johnson AFB, North Carolina. *J. Ethell*

Top right: Like the masters of a great theatre organ, the BUFF's pilots play the machine with surprising ease. Note the TV screens for the EVS (eletro-optical viewing system) hooked to the TV and IR sensors. *J. Ethell*

Centre right: The aircraft in which one of the authors flew, 58-0170, taxies out for the mission from Seymour Johnson AFB, North Carolina. This 68th Bomb Wing Stratofort had 8,058.2 airframe hours on it at the start. *J. Ethell*

Right: 0170 just after getting airborne at Seymour. This G model still has a great deal of life in her. *J. Ethell*

'penetrate' airspace protected by 'enemy' fighters, in this case F-106 Delta Darts flown by pilots of the 119th Fighter Interceptor Squadron from Atlantic City, New Jersey. 1,000ft off the waves, we had a chance to handle the aircraft in evasive manoeuvres as the 106s made their runs. Although limited to banks of 30° (which would not be wartime manoeuvring), the BUFF does quite well for such a truck of an airplane. The ECM gear and the gunner's radar were working overtime with some real targets and the training proved quite valuable. The Darts still managed to shoot us down a few times but we got them a few times as well.

Even though the SAC lunches and coffee are quite good, after over seven hours cramped into the small spaces of the B-52, lunch was a gourmet's delight. Sitting for so long is quite fatiguing and one's rear end tends to go numb. Being preoccupied with the mission, one almost forgets how uncomfortable sitting in one spot for long periods can be.

By 1545hr the BUFF was heading back for Seymour and home. Since two co-pilots were aboard for qualification, the decision was made to practice touch and go landings. With the spoilers out on the wings as air brakes, the ailerons become quite sensitive – at least compared to what they are like normally. A new BUFF pilot tends to get into a little overcontrolling the first time he flies the aircraft in this configuration but the impression is one of delight at the transformation.

Holding normal approach and final speeds for the aircraft is not difficult but no wing low for crosswind landings – the steerable landing gear trucks allow the aircraft to be crabbed into the wind with the main gear wheels pointing straight down the runway.

Once the aircraft is over the numbers, power is chopped. The pilot then flares the monster so that the trucks hit equally on touchdown. If the forward wheels hit first, the aircraft rebounds into the air . . . if the rearward wheels hit first, the aircraft slams down onto the runway. As the co-pilots aboard took turns, a few hard landings kicked the generators off line and lit up the master caution light. It obviously takes a great deal of skill to set all that weight down on two points fore and aft at the same time.

SAC crews work hard, long hours. Nowhere is that more evident than in the aircraft and on alert. Presently debate continues over the life extension of the B-52, another manned bomber as a follow on . . . perhaps a derivative of the B-1 or the F-111 or an entirely new aircraft . . . and the possibiity of ending the manned bomber programme entirely. Regardless of the outcome, it seems the Boeing Stratofortress will be in the US arsenal for some time to come, far outlasting its original projected service life.

Appendices

Chronology

June 1946	Boeing awarded preliminary design contract for new global bomber.
June 1948	Air Force internal opposition to B-52 concept ends with Berlin Blockade.
15 March 1951	Boeing received Air Force 'Letter of Intent' for B-52 production tooling.
29 November 1951	Roll-out of XB-52.
15 March 1952	Roll-out of YB-52.
15 April 1952	First flight of YB-52.
2 October 1952	First flight of XB-52.
28 September 1953	Wichita named as second source for B-52 production.
18 March 1954	First B-52A roll-out.
5 August 1954	First flight of B-52A at Seattle.
25 January 1955	First flight of B-52B at Seattle.
29 June 1955	First B-52 delivered to SAC's 93rd Bomb Wing, Castle AFB, California.
7 December 1955	First Wichita-buit B-52 rolled-out.
9 March 1956	First flight of B-52C at Seattle.
14 May 1956	First flight of B-52D at Wichita.
14 June 1956	Delivery of first B-52D to Castle AFB from Wichita.
27 August 1956	Boeing given preliminary authorisation for B-52G production.
28 September 1956	First flight of B-52D at Seattle.
25 November 1956	Eight B-52s complete record non-stop flights of up to 17,000 miles taking them over the North Pole.
6 December 1956	Announcement made that B-52 to be awarded Collier Trophy for 1956.
18 January 1957	Three B-52s land at March AFB after flying around the world in 45hr 19min. Average speed 530mph for the 24,325 miles.
3 October 1957	First flight of B-52E at Seattle.
17 October 1957	First flight of B-52E at Wichita.
17 November 1957	Six B-52s land at Plattsburgh AFB, NY after flying non-stop round trip between the United States and Buenos Aires, Argentina in 21hr 42min.
6 May 1958	First flight of B-52F at Seattle.
14 May 1958	First flight of B-52F at Wichita.
23 July 1958	First B-52G rolled-out at Wichita.
27 October 1958	First B-52G flight.
1 November 1958	First B-52G delivered to Air Research & Development Command.
15 December 1958	Record non-stop, 18-hour unrefuelled flight of more than 9,000 miles completed by a B-52G.
!3 February 1959	First B-52G delivered to SAC, Travis AFB, California.
25 February 1959	Last Seattle-built B-52 (an F model) deliverd to Air Force.
1 August 1959	A B-52G landed at Edwards AFB, California to complete a 28-hour non-stop flight over all state capitals, including Alaska.
4 September 1959	Boeing Wichita receives production go-ahead for the B-52H Model.
2 March 1960	A SAC crew from Eglin AFB, Florida is first to launch both Hound Dog missiles on a single flight.
12 April 1960	A B-52G flew from Eglin AFB to the North Pole and returned to the Atlantic missile range to score a successful Hound Dog launch. The 22-hour flight covered 10,800 miles non-stop.
23 September 1960	Last B-52G rolled-out at Wichita.
30 September 1960	First B-52H rolled-out at Wichita.
14 December 1960	SAC B-52G crew flew 10,000-mile circuit from Edwards AFB non-stop and without refuelling.
16 March 1961	First B-52H flight at Wichita.
9 May 1961	First B-52H delivered to SAC at Wurtsmith AFB, Michigan.
11 January 1962	A B-52H from Minot AFB flew 12,519 non-stop miles from Kadena Air Base, Okinawa to Torrejon Air Base, Madrid,

	Spain in 21hr 52min to set or break 11 distance, course and speed records without refuelling.
6-7 June 1962	SAC B-52H flew 11,303 miles unrefuelled from Seymour Johnson AFB, North Carolina over North America and return.
22 June 1962	Last B-52H roll-out, ending production programme that dated back to November 1951.
26 October 1962	Last B-52H officially delivered to SAC at Minot AFB, North Dakota.
18 June 1965	B-52s stationed on Guam strike targets in Vietnam for first time.
11 May 1966	First high-density B-52D bomber strikes against North Vietnamese targets.
29 June 1966	Last of B-52Bs placed in extended storage.
7 April 1967	U-Tapao AFB, Thailand activated for B-52 operations.
4 August 1972	First SRAM-equipped B-52s operational.
24 June 1973	First B-52H equipped with EVS delivered to K.I. Sawyer AFB.
15 August 1973	Final SAC B-52 mission over South-East Asia.
21 February 1974	First B-52H equipped with Phase IV ECM delivered to Grand Forks AFB.
25 February 1977	Last of 80 B-52Ds returned to duty following 'Pacer Plank' structural modification to extend service life.

Specifications

	Models B-52A to B-52	**B-52G**	**B-52H**
Take-off Weight:	Over 450,000lb	Over 488,000lb	Over 488,000lb
Speed:	650mph	650mph	650mph
Number of Engines:	Eight	Eight	Eight
Thrust per Engine: (All Pratt & Whitney)	Over 10,000lb J57-P-1W, J57-P-29W J57-P-19W, JP-57-P-43W	Over 10,000lb J57-P-43WB	Over 17,000lb TF33-P-3 Turbofans
Unrefuelled Range:	Over 6,000 miles	Over 7,500 miles	Over 10,000 miles
Altitude:	Over 50,000ft	Over 50,000ft	Over 50,000ft
Armament:	Four .50 cal machine guns	Four .50 cal machine guns	20mm Gatling cannon
Wingspan:	185ft	185ft	185ft
Sweepback:	35°	35°	35°
Length:	156ft	160ft	164ft
Tail Height:	48ft	40ft 8in	40ft 8in
Crew:	Six	Six	Six
Bomb Load:	Over 20,000lb*	Over 20,000lb**	Over 20,000lb*

*Modified B-52D 60,000lb

**20 Cruise missiles; six on each pylon plus eight internal.

Model Differences

Model	Fire control	Bomb/nav system	Engine	Static thrust	External fuel	Total fuel
XB-52	none	none	J57-P-3	8,800lb	1,000gal	38,865gal
YB-52	none	none	J57-P-3	8,800lb	1,000gal	38,865gal
B-52A	A-3A	none	J57-P-1W	10,000lb	1,000gal	37,550gal
B-52B	A-3A MD-5	M-6A	J57-P-1W J57-P-19 J57-P-29W J57-P-29WA	10,000lb 12,100lb 12,100lb 12,100lb	1,000gal (jettisonable)	37,550gal
B-52C	A-3A	AN/ASQ-48(V) AN/ASB-15 AN/APN-108 MD-1	J57-P-19W J57-P-29WA	12,100lb	3,000gal	41,550gal
B-52D	MD-9	Same as C except that internal structural mods added 921lb				
B-52E	MD-9	AN/ASQ-38(V) AN/ASB-4A AN/APN-89A MD-1 AJA-1	J57-P-19W J57-P-29W	12,100lb	3,000gal	41,550gal
B-52F	MD-9	Same as E	J57-P-43W J57-P-43WA J57-P-43WB	13,750lb	3,000gal	41,550gal
B-52G	AN/ASG-15	AN/ASQ-38(V) AN/ASB-16 AN/APN-89A MD-1 AJA-1	J57-P-43W J57—P-43WB	13,750lb	700gal (fixed)	47,975gal
B-52H	AN/ASG-15	AN/ASQ-38(V) AN/ASB-9A AN/APN-89A MD-1 AJN-8 J-4	TF33-P-1 TF33-P-3	16,000lb 17,000lb†	700gal	47,975gal

The B-52 cruises in the vicinity of 600mph, depending upon several variables, including altitude, temperature, and external stores carried. Its speed is approximately 620mph at 20,000ft or .84 Mach. Unrefuelled range at optimum altitude is 8,000 miles for the G model, and 10% to 15% greater for the H model (due to its more fuel-efficient turbofan engines). Service ceiling is 55,000ft. Weapons carried externally degrade performance.

The vertical tail was cut-down, integral-fuel wing introduced, and gunner moved forward in the G and H models. The B-52G retains four .50 calibre guns; the H model is fitted with a 20mm Gatling cannon which fires at the rate of 6,000 rounds/min.

Right and overleaf: Line drawings showing basic external differences between B-52D, the B-52G and the B-52H. *Boeing*

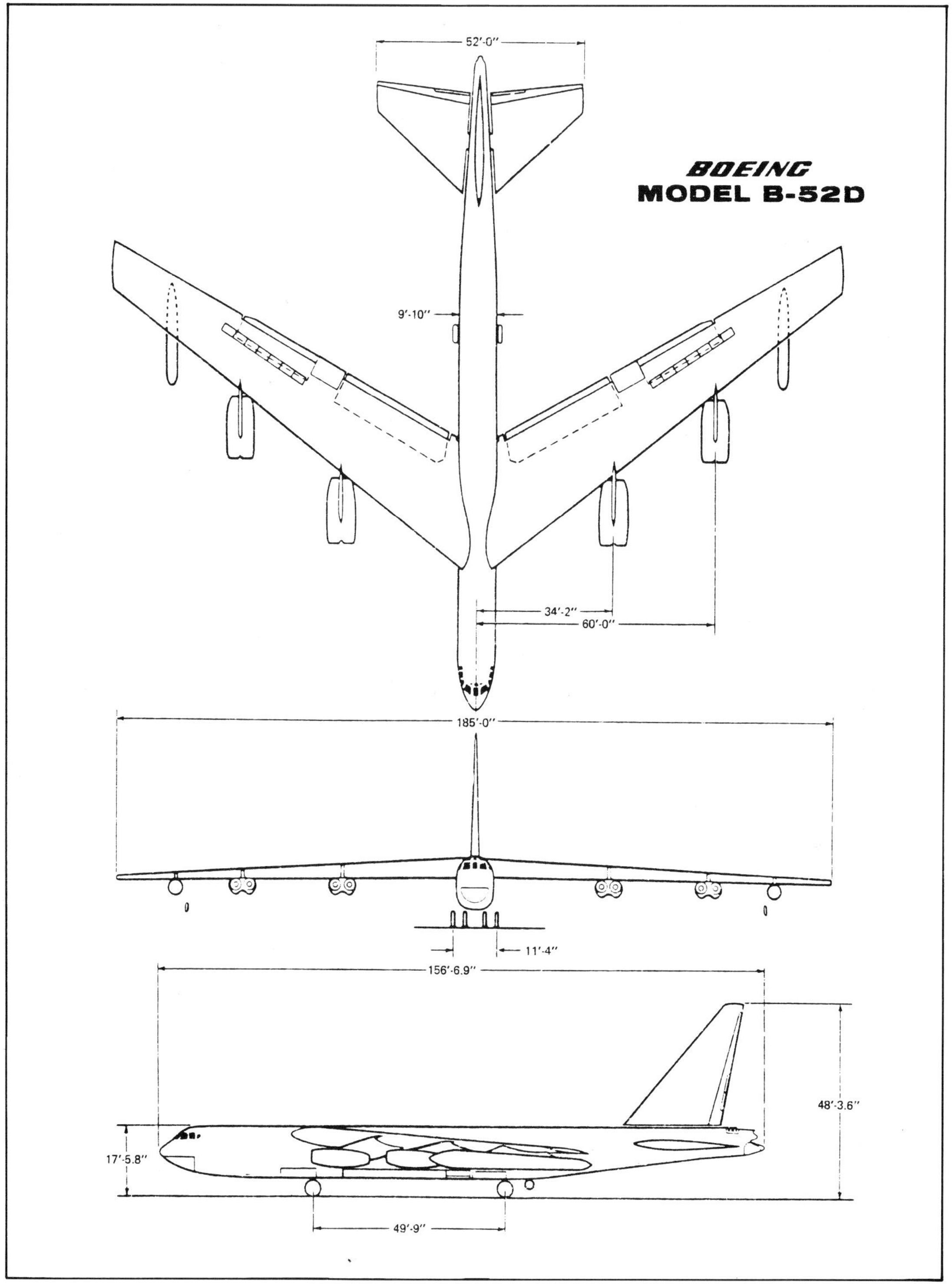
BOEING
MODEL B-52D
52'-0"
9'-10"
34'-2"
60'-0"
185'-0"
11'-4"
156'-6.9"
48'-3.6"
17'-5.8"
49'-9"

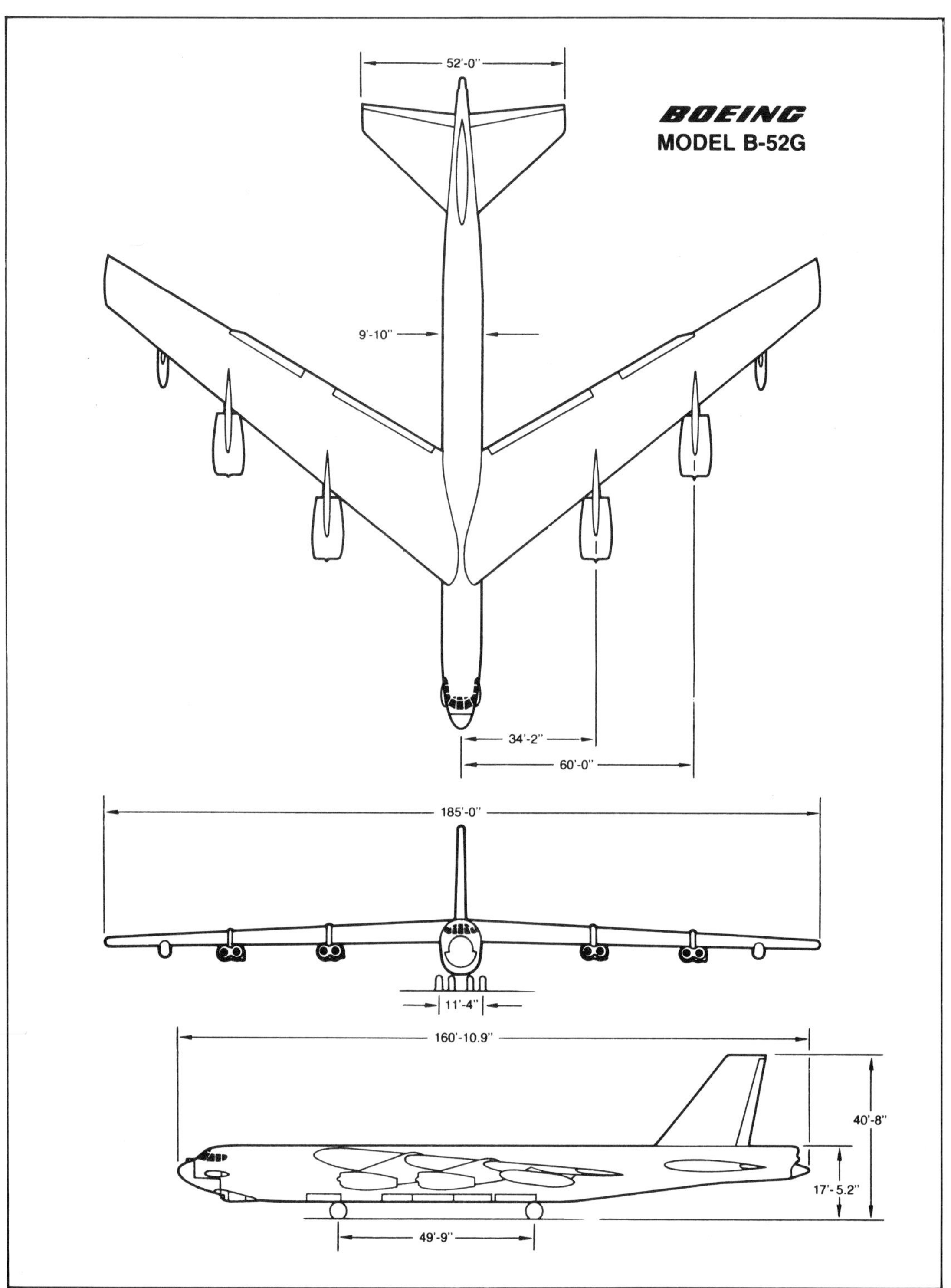
BOEING
MODEL B-52G
52'-0"
9'-10"
34'-2"
60'-0"
185'-0"
11'-4"
160'-10.9"
40'-8"
17'-5.2"
49'-9"

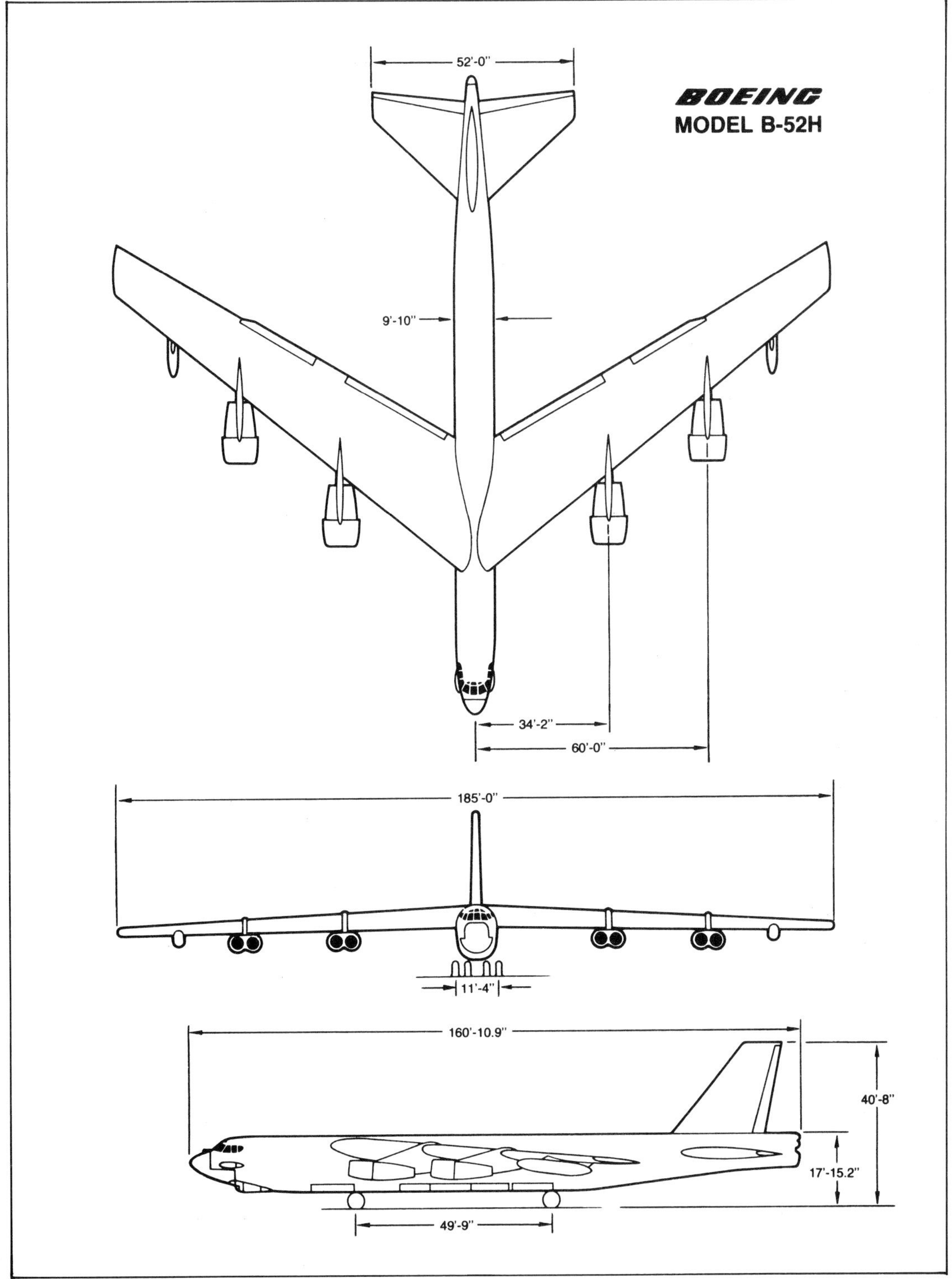
BOEING
MODEL B-52H
52'-0"
9'-10"
34'-2"
60'-0"
185'-0"
11'-4"
160'-10.9"
40'-8"
17'-15.2"
49'-9"

Operational B-52 Units and Bases

I Eighth Air Force—Barksdale AFB, LA
A 19th Air Division—Carswell AFB, TX
1 2nd Bombardment Wing, B-52G, Barksdale AFB, LA
2 7th Bombardment Wing, B-52D, Carswell AFB, TX
B 40th Air Division—Wurtsmith AFB, MI
1 379th Bombardment Wing, B-52G, Wurtsmith AFB, MI
2 410th Bombardment Wing, B-52H, K.I. Sawyer AFB, MI
C 42nd Air Division—Blytheville AFB, AR
1 19th Bombardment Wing, B-52G, Robins AFB, GA
2 68th Bombardment Wing, B-52G, Seymour Johnson AFB, NC
3 97th Bombardment Wing, B-52G, Blytheville AFB, AR
D 45th Air Division—Pease AFB, NH
1 42nd Bombardment Wing, B-52G, Loring AFB, ME (moved in 1979)
2 416th Bombardment Wing, B-52G, Griffis AFB, NY

II Fifteenth Air Force—March AFB, CA
A 4th Air Division—F.E. Warren AFB, WY
1 28th Bombardment Wing, B-52H, Ellsworth AFB, SD
B 12th Air Division—Dyess AFB, TX
1 22nd Bombardment Wing, B-52D, March AFB, CA
2 96th Bombardment Wing, B-52D, Dyess AFB, TX
C 14th Air Division—Beale AFB, CA
1 320th Bombardment Wing, B-52G, Mather AFB, CA
2 93rd Bombardment Wing, B-52G/h, Castle AFB, CA
D 47th Air Division—Fairchild AFB, WA
1 92nd Bombardment Wing, B-52G, Fairchild AFB, WA
E 57th Air Division—Minot AFB, ND
1 5th Bombardment Wing, B-52H, Minot AFB, ND
2 319th Bombardment Wing, B-52H, Grand Forks, ND

III Third Air Division—Andersen AFB, Guam
A 60th Bombardment Squadron, B-52D, Andersen AFB, Guam

Production/Deliveries

Model	AF serial	Initial delivery	Max/empty weight (lb)
XB-52	49-230	4/53	405,000
YB-52	49-231	3/53	405,000
B-52A	52-001—003	6/54	420,000/167,500
B-52B	52-004—013	9/54	420,000/170,000
	52-8710—8716	6/55	
	53-366—376	8/55	
	53-377—398	11/55	
B-52C	53-399—408	4/56	450,000/170,800
B-52D	55-010—117	10/56	450,000/171,700
	55-673—680		
	56-580—630		
	56-657—698		
B-52E	56-631—656	11/57	450,000/172,600
	56-699—712		
	57-014—029		
	57-095—138		
B-52F	57-030—073	5/58	450,000/170,200
	57-139—183		
B-52G	57-6468—6520	10/58	488,000/164,000
	58-158—258		
	59-2564—2602		
B-52H	60-001—070	3/61	488,000/165,500
	61-001—0032		

Right: A B-52G refuelling from a KC-135 Stratotanker. *USAF*

Above right: The KC-135 is turning out to be the real workhorse of Strategic Air Command now that it has been modified to extend its service life. It will be right up there with the B-52 for the next several decades, most likely longer. *Boeing*

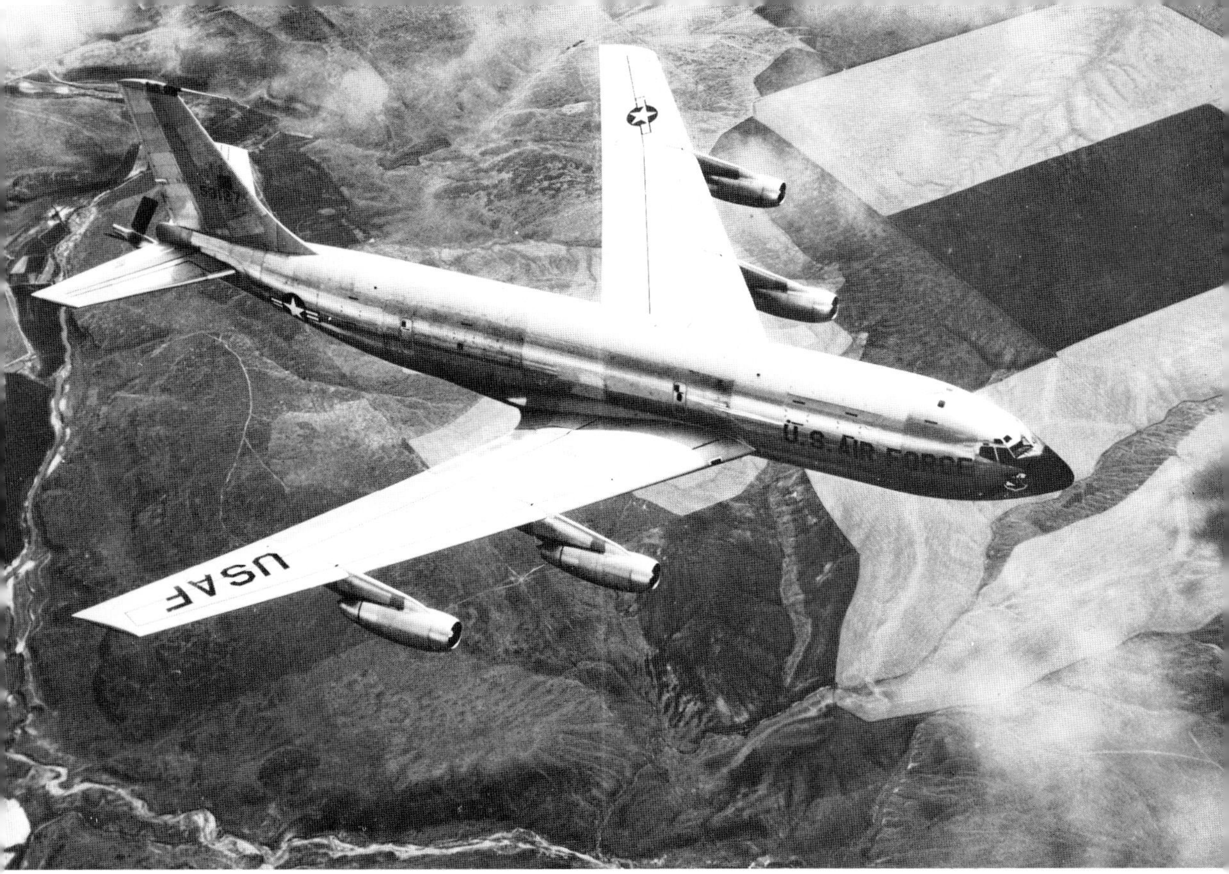
USAF
U.S. AIR FORCE

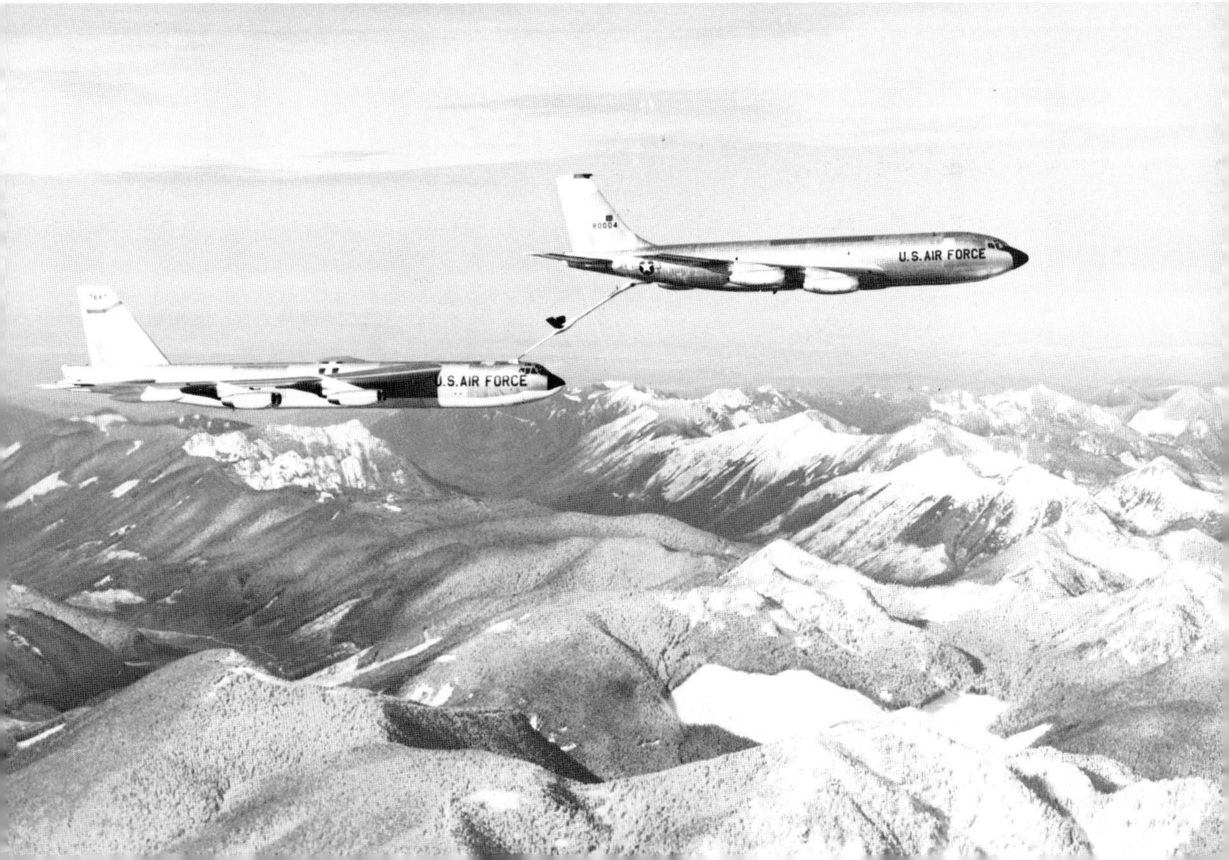
80004
U.S. AIR FORCE
U.S. AIR FORCE

KC-135A Stratotanker

The Strategic Air Command received its first KC-135A on 31 January 1957, with the 93rd Air Refuelling Squadron putting its first plane in operational service on 28 June 1957.

The Air Force announced its intention to purchase an undisclosed number of the tankers in August 1954, only a month after the Boeing-financed tanker-transport (707) prototype had made its maiden flight. On 5 October 1954 the official papers for KC-135A production were signed, and just 21 months and 13 days later, on 18 July 1956, the first production aircraft rolled from the factory at Renton, Washington, following by only a few moments the 888th and last of the KC-97 tankers it succeeded. The KC-135 made its first flight on 31 August 1956.

Designed for high-speed, high altitude refuelling, the KC-135A is equipped with a telescoping flying boom. Aerial refuelling equipment is all on the lower deck, leaving the upper deck clear for cargo or troop carrying use. This deck can accommodate 80 passengers or 25 tons of cargo, or a combination of both.

In addition to the 732 KC-135As built, Boeing produced another 88 similar craft for other Air Force uses such as flying command posts, pure transports, electronic reconnaissance and photo-mapping. The last of these special purpose aircraft was delivered to the USAF in late 1966.

On 12 February 1976 a programme was begun to completely re-skin the wings of the KC-135 fleet. Then on 10 June 1977 Boeing Wichita (the Boeing Wichita Division became the Boeing Wichita Company) received a contract to design, install and flight-test a set of winglets on a KC-135A. The near-vertical winglets on each wingtip transform the drag-producing tip vortices into lift/thrust forces to increase range and/or fuel economy. While these programmes were in progress, on 13 January 1978 the Air Force awarded Boeing Wichita a contract for a data study on re-engining the KC-135A Stratotankers. The KC-135s will obviously be around as long as the B-52s remain operational.

KC-135A Specification

Span: 130ft 10in
Length: 136ft 3in
Tail height: 38ft 4in
Sweepback: 35°
Gross weight: 297,000lb
Engines: Four P&W J57 turbojets of 13,750lb thrust each
Cruising speed: 600mph
Range: 5,000 statue miles (normal load)
Service ceiling: 41,000ft
Crew: Four (pilot, co-pilot, navigator, boom operator)

B-52 Offensive Avionics Systems (OAS)

A full-scale devlopment contract valued at $129million was awarded to the Boeing Wichita Company in August 1978 sponsored by the Air Force Systems Command's Aeronautical Systems Division (ASD) at Wright-Patterson AFB, Ohio. Completion of this programme was expected in February 1982.

The contract provided for fabrication, integration and test of selected subsystems to update the offensive avionics for B-52G and H model aircraft and provide an air-launched cruise missile capability for the B-52G.

The goal of the programme is to improve the global bomber's navigation and weapons delivery systems and integrate the cruise missile to meet enemy threats of the 1980s and reduce support costs. Specific avionics improvements include the B-52 weapons delivery system, greater dependability for electronic subsystems with lower operating and maintenance costs, and hardening to nuclear effects.

Major subsystems in the programme include: computers for navigation and weapons delivery; a common strategic Doppler radar being developed by ASD as in input to the inertial navigation system; attitude heading reference system; radar altimeter; terrain correlation; controls and displays, and high accuracy inertial navigation system.

Government furnished equipment for the OAS package includes the Air Force strategic common doppler radar and the Honeywell SPN/GEANS inertial navigation system.

For the remaining OAS subsystems, Boeing selected the following sub-contractors: IBM Federal Systems Division, avionics processors; Lear Siegler Instrument Division, attitude heading reference system; Honeywell Avionics Division, radar altimeter; Sperry Rand's Sperry Flight Systems Division, controls and displays; and Norden Systems of United Technologies, radar modification.

In the OAS programme, Boeing Wichita will equip a B-52G test aircraft with the new avionics by mid-1980. A 12-month flight test programme will follow. The Air Force anticipates initial retrofit of the B-52G and H models with the new OAS starting about mid-1981. Fleet modification is expected to begin about one year later with retrofit of all B-52G and H models. The B-52s will carry gravity bombs, SRAMs, and ALCMs.

Bibliography

Air Force History, Office of; *The United States Air Force in Southeast Asia*; US Government Printing Office, Washington, DC, 1977.

Air Force History, Office of; *Aces & Aerial Victories*; US Government Printing Office, Washington, DC, 1976.

Air Force History, Office of; *The Battle for the Skies over North Vietnam*; US Government Printing Office, Washington, DC, 1976.

Aviation Week & Space Technology; Numerous articles on B-52; McGraw-Hill, New York, Inc.

Day, Bonner; 'The B-52: Growing More Vital With Age', *Air Force Magazine*; February 1979, pp32-37.

Drendel, Lou; *B-52 Stratofortress in Action*; Squadron/Signal Publications, Inc, 1975.

Drenkowski, Dana K.; 'Operation Linebacker II', *Soldier of Fortune Magazine* (1977).

Ellis, Gen Richard H.; 'Strategic Nuclear Deterrent Overview Statement', *FY 80 Budget Authorization Hearing Before the Sentate Armed Services Committee* by Commander in Chief, SAC; 1 February 1979.

Ethell, Jeffrey L.; 'In The Buff', *Air Progress Aviation Review*; Fall 1977, pp82-85.

Holder, William G.; *Boeing B-52 Stratofortress*; Aero Publishers, Inc, Fallbrook, 1975.

Strategic Air Command; *Development of Strtategic Air Command* 1946-1976; Office of the Historian, Offutt AFB, 1976.

Strategic Air Command; *Soviet Military Capabiities*; HQ SAC, Offutt, AFB, 1979.

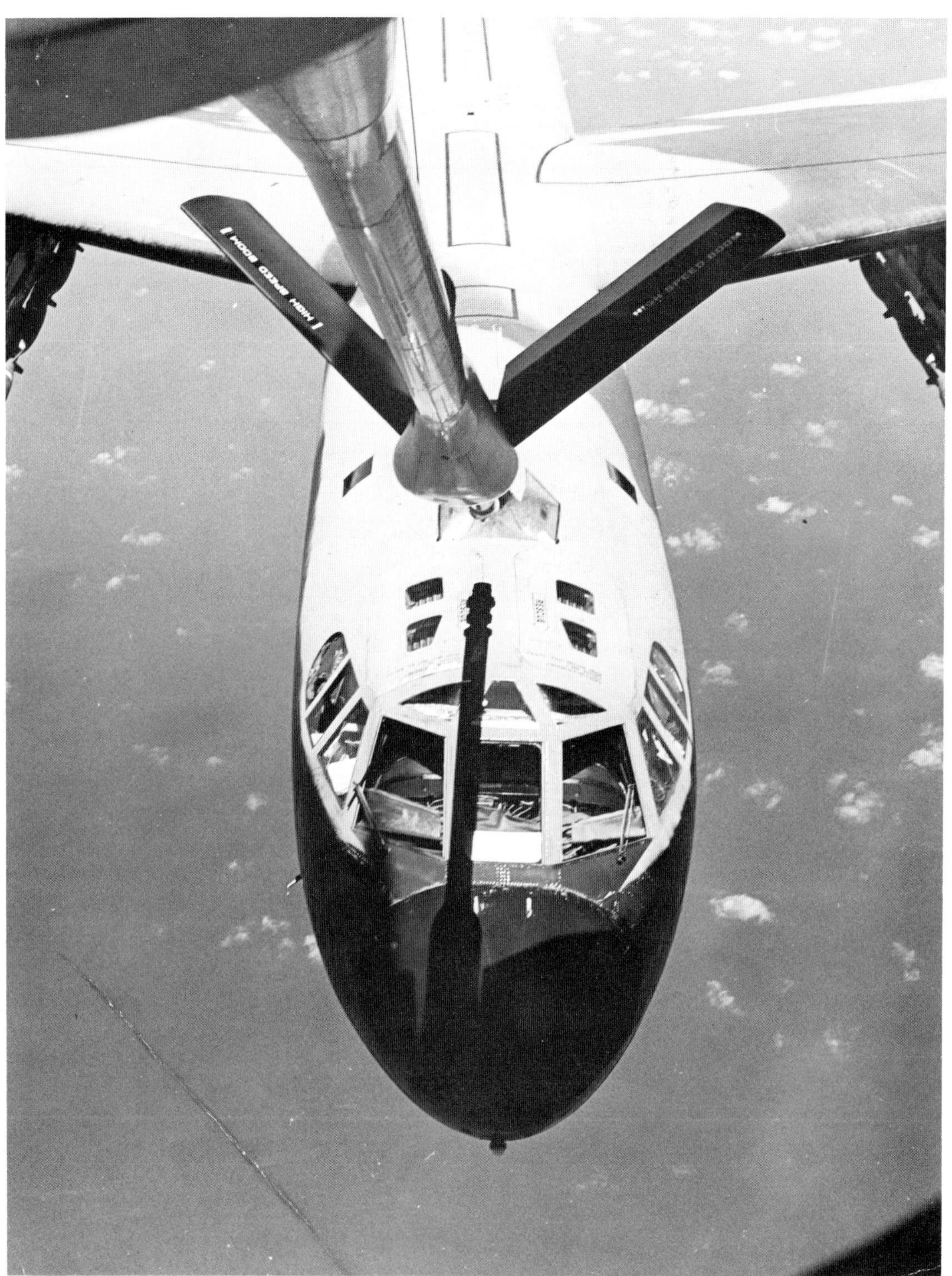
HIGH SPEED BOOM
HIGH SPEED BOOM